Shift...
or Get off the Pot

26 Simple Truths About Getting A Life

Linda Edgecombe

INSOMNIAC PRESS

Library and Archives Canada Cataloguing in Publication

Edgecombe, Linda, 1960-
    Shift or get off the pot : simple truths about getting a life / Linda Edgecombe.

ISBN 978-1-897178-65-2

    1. Self-evaluation. 2. Change (Psychology). 3. Self-actualization (Psychology). I. Title.

BF637.C5E34 2008   158.1   C2008-904292-1

The publisher gratefully acknowledges the support of the Department of Canadian Heritage through the Book Publishing Industry Development Program.

Printed and bound in Canada

Insomniac Press
192 Spadina Avenue, Suite 403
Toronto, Ontario, Canada, M5T 2C2
www.insomniacpress.com

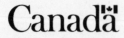

It's Time!

Advance Praise for *Linda's Message!*

"Your speech was dynamic and energizing and even though you were near the end of a busy three days, you got everyone listening and actively involved in what you were saying. It was fantastic and I can't tell you how much we appreciate your helping us finish our WON Conference on such a high note. After hearing you speak it is obvious why you are in such high demand as a keynote speaker. Thanks so much for helping us make our conference a huge success."
~ **McDonald's Restaurants Women Operators Week**

"Linda was an overwhelming success for our organization. Everyone had a wonderful time listening to Linda's words— she made us think and renew ourselves—all the while laughing and enjoying every minute of her presentation! Energy, perspective, and fun—those are the resounding feelings that we received from Linda."
~ **Shell Oil**

"I get a LOT of newsletters sent to me....and I appreciate them and almost always reply with 'very nice! Keep up the good work! But please take me off the list.' Linda....please KEEP me on your list. This is a very kick ass newsletter!"
~ **Joe Calloway, professional speaker and business trainer**

"Your enthusiastic and enlightening discussion on 'life perspectives' helped to set the tone for the entire conference."
~ **National Paperbox Association**

Dedication

This book is dedicated to everyone who wants their life back. You already know what needs to be done and just need a good kick in the pants. So let this book serve as your proverbial kick.

Before you start the book

Turn to page 129 and answer the question there. Then come back to this page and proceed.
Looking forward to your emails.

Linda Mae
www.lindaedgecombe.com
email me at info@lindaedgecombe.com

Table of Contents

Introduction

Note to Self: Snap Out of It!

Some phrases take on a life of their own.

They mean so many things on so many levels; they just can't go back into the box after first being uttered. They work too well. In fact, they work so well we just can't stop using them.

These sayings have been around so long, are so entirely commonplace, so overused and misunderstood even, that we barely heed their call anymore. Sure, you can add as many exclamation points and capital letters and as much boldface type as you want, but the message still doesn't get through.

Some phrases deserve a closer look.

"Snap out of it!"

We hear it all the time.

The careworn mother to her petulant teen, "Snap out of it!"

The frazzled coach to his fumbling receiver, "Snap out of it!"

The knowing teacher to her Monday morning homeroom, "Snap out of it!"

The boss to his employee, the employee to the assistant, the assistant to the coworker, the coworker to the coffee boy, the coffee boy to the customer, the driver to the toll booth operator, the customer to the cashier, the husband to the wife, the wife to the husband, "Snap out of it!"

What is *it* exactly?

What is *it* that we need to snap out of? Or where is *it* we need to snap away from? How is it that we forget what we already know? Is it possible we come into this world with all the information we need to become our best selves, successful and happy? Is it possible that the *it* we're snapping out of is the problem and where we're snapping back *to* is the solution?

Seriously, what would happen if we could unclutter our minds, calm down, and get back to square one? How much could you accomplish without all the mental junk that follows you around from day to day? The negative self-talk, depressing internal dialogue, the fear and the self-loathing and the insecurity and the endless, ceaseless, needless drama?

Aren't you sick of *it*?

Well, then, "Snap out of it!" I'm serious about this. I wrote this book to remind you that you already have all the answers you need to become who you are supposed to be in this lifetime. They're just tucked away somewhere.

Perhaps it's in these "tucked away" places that *it* exists. For most of the population it is a safe yet unsatisfying place to live one's life. We live here in it and go about our daily lives unaware that just beneath the surface of us lies a person who is screaming to come to life, literally shouting, "Snap out of it!"

If only we could hear it.

If only we would listen.

Now, don't get me wrong here: this may sound all hazy and "out there" but it's not. This is simple stuff and that's what this book is about. It's about remembering what you already know; it's about finding *the simple truths about what it takes to get a life and be happy.*

So what are simple truths? Truths are things and states of being, ones that all of us bring into the world that can't be disputed or argued with. The question I want to answer in this book is: how can you mine the truths that will bring you closer to yourself? The "why you are here" questions. Now, don't get all soft on me now, because self-awareness has never been this painless.

This book is a pain-free, self-guided tour back to square one. It's a journey back to the core of you, the place where you can meet yourself, know yourself, love yourself, and get on with the job of learning *the simple truth about what it takes to get a life and be happy.*

Life can be a mystery, but unlike a mystery writer I'm going to let you take a peek at the end here, at the beginning. That's right; let's start at the finish and answer the burning question: Are you really *happy?*

Note to Self:

I wrote this book to remind you that you already have all the answers you need to become who you are supposed to be in this lifetime. They're just tucked away, waiting to be discovered.

Section 1

Disconnect to Re-Engage!
It's time you got to know you again.

Overview:
Back away from the cellphone!

OK people, put down your cellphones, PDAs, pocket PCs...whatever! And *focus*. This may sound amusing but I am dead serious here. I don't mean turn them to vibrate, stun, or whatever setting you normally use to appear courteous. I want you to shut them *off*. Off means *off*. But wait, there's more: I want you to keep it off for one full day. Yes indeed, I formally declare the first ever "National Disconnect to Re-engage Day." So how do you know if you need this challenge? Well, if you have checked for messages in the past ten minutes, you need to detox. If you have ever scrolled emails over the dinner table, you need to detox. If you have checked messages and emails while on vacation, right after making love to your partner, while the kids opened their Christmas gifts, or during your weekly visit to church, you need to detox. If you simply own one, you need to detox.

We all need to feel important. We need that "I'm needed" feeling we get when our little personal excitement device vibrates on our hip. I can feel the list of reasons coming up why *you* are different from the other two billion connection crutch addicts, but to tell you the truth, you are not. Now if you are currently working in an Emergency department, are an "on call" doc or EMT, then you can keep yours on during your day off. For the rest of you who are thinking, "what if... someone really needs me?" tell them they can call you on your land line and if you are not there, *leave a message*.

Now take the free time you will have on this day and go buy yourself a stamp, put pen to paper, and write someone a handwritten letter. You may need a hand massage afterwards to help with the cramps you will experience, but the person you write to will love receiving your letter later in the week.

Here's the real reason you are going to take on this challenge: I want you to "just notice what you notice" about yourself for one full day. Notice how you love the freedom from the constant connection; notice that you feel out of sorts and seem to fumble around; notice what people actually look like when they talk with you this day; notice what you can read between the lines in conversations with family, friends, and co-workers. Most importantly, notice yourself. Being engaged in something, whether it's your work, your relationships, or yourself, means having a current, conscious awareness of more than just the obvious. It means giving a damn about what you are doing and consciously making decisions to give it your all. Here's to shifting towards Re-engagement.

Simple Shift #1

Pick a Lane
Reduce the Number of Roles You Play

Herbert Hoover once said, "About the time we can make ends meet, somebody moves the ends." What about you? Does it feel like someone is constantly moving the ends on your success? The more roles we take on, the more life becomes like those heat shimmers just in front of us as we drive down the road on a hot summer day. Every time we think we're getting close and going to drive right through them, they pop up just a little further down the road.

That promotion you were supposed to get last week gets put off until next month. The dishwasher you had on layaway—and were supposed to collect tomorrow—won't be yours until a few weeks' worth of tomorrows because your car got a flat on the way to pick it up. Those last five pounds you want to lose just became those last ten pounds—thanks to the holidays.

Life has a way of moving the finish line for us. The minute we get over one hill there are three more we didn't know about until we got to the top and looked down. This corner leads to that corner, and that corner leads to the next bend.

Where did the finish line go?

Well, maybe we could run a little faster—and go a little further—if we didn't bring so much baggage to the starting line. Think about all the roles you play from day to day: provider, homemaker, father, daughter, brother, sister, entertainer, listener, speaker, referee, and judge. No wonder you can't see the finish line—there are too many people in your way!

In this section I want you to think about all those roles you play and consider whether they are helping you—or hurting you. Ask yourself, "Am I doing the best I can, considering everything that's going on for me?"

Notice I didn't say are you the best, I said, are you *doing* the best. Even with that careful caveat, most of us hold our cards close to our chests, because for some reason we think if anyone finds out we really have no idea what we're doing, we'll fail for sure.

The truth of the matter is: *none* of us has it together.

Most of us suffer from what I call "imposter syndrome." We don't just "fake it 'til we make it," we plain old fake it all the time: 24/7/365. In the privacy of your own home, as you reflect on your day-to-day life, can you say on most days that you did the best you could *considering* everything that's going on for you right now?

Note to Self:

In this section I want you to think about all those roles you play and consider whether you they are helping you—or hurting you.

Are you doing the best you can, considering everything that's going on for you?

The part of this equation to focus on is "... *considering* everything that's going on for you." Think about the complexity of what you've got going on right now. Parent, sister, brother, sandwich maker, story teller and homework taskmaster, taxi driver, first aid attendant, cook, grocery shopper, friend, lover, boss, frontline worker, coach, Brownie or Cub Scout leader, church member, and so on.

Most of us pile so much "stuff" on our plates that it has become hard to breathe, let alone take a bite! It would be easy to blame the world at large for our overabundance of duties, but the truth is we have only ourselves to blame. We think that by taking on so much, we're actually contributing to the betterment of whatever we are saying "yes" to. But actually, I believe we pile so much on our plates that the "pile" itself becomes an out.

We set ourselves up for failure because we're taking on many more tasks and then backing out, using the excuse that we are overwhelmed and overworked. And others will wonder how we could possibly do all the stuff we've taken on? But in the meantime, even as we struggle with our sanity, let alone our success, we look "great" to the outside world and come off as such a giving person who's there for everyone.

Everyone, that is, but ourselves.

Let me suggest that it's time to make a few priorities in your life. Ask yourself this question, "What am I doing that truly brings me joy and energy?" That is the "stuff" you should be concentrating on. If you actually enjoy carting the kids around to soccer practice and dance class and spelling bees, if that gives you some together time and you love the teamwork and camaraderie, more power to you. Load it on!

But if you cringe at planning the office party every year, why would you ever commit to it in the first place? Do you think you'll get fired if you say no? Do you think you're the only one who can do it? Do you think you're the one who does it *best*? Maybe there's someone waiting in the wings just dying to take over for you. Why not give him or her a chance?

Embrace those duties that truly bring you joy and add to your life. Strongly consider letting go of the others. Now, I know if parenting is draining you right now, this is one you can't necessarily let go of, but could you do it slightly differently?

For instance, let's say you're like nearly every other parent out there and you *don't* enjoy ferrying your kids around to fifteen extracurricular activities per week. How can you reduce that number by five activities, or maybe even by half? Can you share transport duties with other parents? Can your child concentrate on a couple of activities she really loves? Try using the "c" word once in awhile and *compromise*— you, your children, your spouse, your co-workers, your neighbours will all be better off when you do "less stuff, more better!"

Note to Self:

It would be easy to blame the world at large for our over-abundance of duties, but the truth is we have only ourselves to blame.

Step 1:
Ranking the Roles You Play

They say life is a buffet: a free-for-all that we are encouraged to sample to our heart's content. But what usually happens at a buffet? We stand there like a deer in the headlights, overwhelmed by all the possibilities. Then we shift from "deer in the headlights" to "kid in a candy store," grabbing everything in sight, just to make sure we get it all in. Later, we're in what I call the "antacid phase," looking high and low for the bottle of Tums!

When we say "yes" to everyone else to the point where we have to say "no" to ourselves, there is no antacid strong enough to drown out all the resulting stress and resentment we feel.

To help you take a few of those "junk food" items off your plate of current responsibilities, I'm including this quick exercise to help you prioritize the roles you play—and how they affect you. The following are several roles we take on in our lives, for better or worse. Go through each one and rate whether the role is an energizing or draining one in your life right now. Yes, some will be both energizing and draining, and a few roles you can't get out of, but being aware of the roles and how they affect your energy is a start on the road to a healthier you!

Role	Energizes me	Drains me
Parent	_____	_____
Sibling	_____	_____
Daughter/ Son	_____	_____
Carer	_____	_____

Role	Energizes me	Drains me
Friend	_____	_____
Volunteer	_____	_____
Service club member	_____	_____
Church member	_____	_____
Athlete	_____	_____
Boss	_____	_____
Artist	_____	_____
Crafts- person	_____	_____
Driver	_____	_____
Neighbourhood cook	_____	_____
Business partner	_____	_____
Part-time worker	_____	_____
Student	_____	_____
Babysitter	_____	_____
Other	_____	_____

Note to Self:

Choose three roles on your list that no longer give you joy and plan a guilt-free exit strategy. Trust me, you'll love yourself for it. I know you are not going to stop being a parent or family member—just notice if these roles are energizing or draining you right now.

Success Rule # 1
You Can Only Be Successful When You Know WHO and WHAT You Are

Take an honest snapshot of your life. Don't just take your "best side" and smile at the pretty picture in the frame: use the wide lens and show yourself, warts and all. Record all that is good, all that could use some improvement, and even the things that need to be discarded entirely.

It's amazing how long we can go just seeing ourselves as we want to be: the capable, helpful, together, hip, cool, friendly, gracious, selfless soul who's always up for just one more favour, task, role, or duty. Meanwhile, we're frazzled to the breaking point, lacking sleep and showing it on every inch of our puffy, exhausted faces. While in our fantasy lives we picture ourselves as king or queen of the prom, in reality we walk around like desperate housewives and Scrooge in our very own melodrama!

I know, I know, it's hard to trust the photographer when you're the one taking the picture. So don't: ask friends and family for an honest assessment as well. Then ask yourself the following eight questions to help discover the true you hiding underneath that big, heaping pile of duties:

1. How would your friends describe you in each of these roles?
2. How would you describe yourself?
3. Which of these roles energize you?
4. What roles would you drop if you could?

5. Can you re-define yourself in any of these roles?
6. Are you truly yourself when you play these roles and are you more *you* in some than in others?
7. Why is that?
8. What do the roles where you are more "yourself" have in common?

The reason I start the book with this lesson is because you really can't go forward unless you know who's taking the journey. In other words, you can only be successful when you know *who* and *what* you are.

Note to Self:

While in our fantasy lives we picture ourselves as king and queen of the prom, in reality we walk around like desperate housewives and Scrooge in our very own melodrama!

Simple Shift #2
Stand on Solid Ground

Understand and Apply Your Values

With so many people depending on us, it's hard to find the time to get to know ourselves—but find the time we must. Since time is limited, it's important to use that time wisely. That is why I've created this quick chart to help you clarify your values and find out exactly where you stand and what you stand for.

Why values? You must know the values you stand for if success and, more importantly, happiness are important to you. Most of us are not clear about our values and we flounder when opportunities come our way. We ask ourselves, "Should I do it or not?" After all, as Wayne Cotton says, "If you know what you want, you can say *no* to what you don't want."

But how can we tell the difference if we don't know the difference? When we are clear about how we see ourselves and the values we operate under, making decisions is easier, quicker, and more beneficial for all involved. Make a list of all the things you find value in, in your home and work life, so that decision-making becomes easier and more satisfying.

Below are a few examples of values you might find important:

Achievement
Friendship
Physical challenge
Advancement and promotion
Personal growth
Adventure
Having a family
Power and authority
Affection (love and caring)
Charity
Privacy
The Arts
Helping society
Public service
Challenging problems
Honesty
Change and variety
Independence
Quality
Close relationships
Influencing others
Quality relationships
Community
Inner harmony
Recognition (respect from others, status)
Competence
Integrity
Religion
Competition
Intellectual status
Reputation
Cooperation

Involvement
Responsibility and accountability
Country
Job tranquility
Security
Creativity
Knowledge
Self-respect
Decisiveness
Leadership
Serenity
Democracy
Location
Sophistication
Ecological awareness
Loyalty
Stability
Economic security
Market position
Effectiveness
Meaningful work
Supervising others
Efficiency
Merit
Time freedom
Ethical practice
Money
Truth
Excellence
Nature
Wealth

Getting on Solid Ground: Simple Steps

1. Choose 20 values from this list and feel free to add your own.
2. Whittle it down to your top ten, then your top five. Now when making decisions daily on your home and work life, reflect on your list. The truth is that when your life feels out of balance, it means you have made priorities that do not match the values you have set for yourself.

    This list-ticking may take time at first—and practice. But don't all good habits?
3. *Now*: in just three minutes, write down the answers to this question, "What do you want to experience in your lifetime?" Don't dilly-dally; do this rapid-fire, no logic, don't over analyze, just write what comes to mind—and heart.
4. Now sit back and look at your list and compare it to your Top Five Values List. Is there conflict between them, or do they align? Do you feel like you are trying to angle park in a parallel universe?
5. The Test: for the next three days, make all of your decisions based on your Top Five Values. This will be challenging. Notice how much more balanced your life feels.

Note to Self:

You do not need to have the same Top Five Values as your spouse or your kids; they should, however, be in the same ballpark.

Simple Shift #3
Survival of the Funniest
The Proper Care and Feeding of
Your Sense of Humour

"If you are going to make an impression, make it a stain"
~ Linda Edgecombe

We've all had a bad-hair day; some of us even have *no*-hair days. You know what I'm talking about, the kind of day where you mess up, screw up, trip up, and cough up that certain, special "something" you wished you hadn't. For these, we tend to beat ourselves up for eternity.

Why did I do that?

What was I thinking?

Will they ever forgive me?

Do they hate me?

Will I ever forgive myself?

And on and on it goes. Some of us hang on to these experiences for a lifetime—and I do mean our *entire* lives. As if that certain someone who remains embedded in your brain from high school or your first job is still thinking about something you said, 10, 15, 25, even 35 years ago.

What's funny about a bad hair day is that, for most of us, it never seems to be very funny at all in the middle of the experience, but later it can be a *great* story to tell. Admit it; despite all the fussing and the fretting, it's a tale to be relived over and over again. At some point, most of us have asked a question we wished we could have shoved back in our mouths as fast as the words were falling out of it.

"When are you due?"

"Is this your granddaughter?"

"Are those real or purchased?"

Okay, I was just *thinking* the last one, but you know what I mean. It's as if in the moment of making a jackass of ourselves, we have some override button that doesn't quite allow us to push the eject button on the shoe in our mouth. But really, in the grand scheme of things, does it really matter?

So often we are still worrying about what other people think when they stopped thinking about us twenty minutes ago—let alone twenty years ago! Be like them; let it go. Mistakes are human; we all make them—we're all forgiven. The point here is to start to laugh at yourself more quickly.

Laughter truly is one of life's strongest medicines. It's a cure-all for whatever ails you—whenever it ails you—and the best part is, it's completely over the counter. You can actually tell when you are getting over issues when you can laugh at yourself.

Don't believe me? Try this one on at your next dinner party: go around the table and ask everyone to share one of their all-time favourite embarrassing moments. It's a great conversation catalyst and if you are up to it, start with yourself. Your story will make it OK for others to tell theirs.

Note to Self:

Everyone has made mistakes, screwed up, said the wrong thing, and has lived to tell the story at the next office party. Find your funny faster; you'll be healthier for it.

Surviving life's embarrassing moments

My favourite flight of any day is what I like to call the "Aqua Velva flight." That is the flight somewhere between about 6:20 am and 8:30 am where you are usually surrounded by the blend of various colognes on the shirts flying to somewhere important, I'm sure.

I got on such a flight a few years back, flying from the west coast to the east coast and, as I like to say, every once in a while the "big guy" gives you a little gift. Well, my friends, that day the gift was sitting right next to me.

He was handsome, had on a beautiful dark suit, and, best of all, he smelled *great*! I mean *great*!!! You see, my husband Kevin has been wearing Stetson cologne for over 20 years now and let's just say I'm a little tired of the old Stetson. My Kevin is a good prairie boy, but after 20 years, I was ready for a change.

Besides, Christmas was coming, so in my head I got the idea to ask this gift sitting next to me what cologne he was wearing. So I leaned toward him and said just that, "Excuse me, I know this is kinda forward, but I'd really like to find out what you've got on?"

He looked at me, got a grin on his face, and said, "Well, to be honest with you, I'm going commando." Now, it probably would have been a good thing if I had known at the time that "going commando" meant he wasn't wearing underwear, but I didn't. You see, it sounded like some kind of sporty, outdoorsy cologne. You know, khaki box, and so on. So then I looked at him and said, "That's great, 'cause I really want to get me some of that!"

Yes, I actually said that. But I didn't even know I was

having a bad hair day; I had no idea I had even embarrassed myself. I was surprised, though, at how flirty he was for the entire flight. Weeks later, I finally found out what "going commando" really meant. So as my face turned red, I thought to myself, *What the heck, another story for the grandkids.*

Note to Self:

He was handsome, had on a beautiful dark suit and, best of all, he smelled great! I mean great!!!

Step 1
Find Your Own Funny Faster
(Lighten Up; Laugh More)

The benefits of having a sense of humour have been well-documented. In fact, numerous studies have been conducted over the years on how laughter and a sense of humour are critical for health, happiness, and well-being. Laughter has been proven to lower blood pressure, decrease the stress hormone cortisol, increase the antibodies that fight infection, protect the heart, improve brain function, and relieve stress.

One thing is for sure: laughter is a universal language that crosses all borders and indicates a bonding connection between people. We have found that both men and women like someone who makes us laugh; a great sense of humour is an attractive quality we look for in our mates.

Think back to the last time you had a side-splitting laugh, where your stomach actually hurt. If you really stop to analyze what was happening, you'll better understand the saying, "hurts so good."

According to the "Science of Laughter" section on the *Discovery Health* website, "When we laugh, natural killer cells which destroy tumors and viruses increase, along with Gamma-interferon (a disease-fighting protein), T-cells (important for our immune system) and B-cells (which make disease-fighting antibodies). As well as lowering blood pressure, laughter increases oxygen in the blood, which also encourages healing."

Elizabeth Scott, MS, who runs the "Stress Management" section of *About.com* explains, "Laughter reduces the level of stress hormones like cortisol, epinephrine, adrenaline, dopamine, and growth hormone. It also increases the level of health-enhancing hormones like endorphins and neurotransmitters."

This release of adrenalin and endorphins does two things for us physically. First, we get energized from a good laugh and, second, we tend to relax after a good laugh with a sigh. As a bonus, this effect reduces any pain we might be feeling.

So here's my advice: if you have had a bad day, bad week, bad month, or bad decade, go home on Friday night and don't rent *Silence of the Lambs* or *Sophie's Choice*. Not that they aren't great movies, but you're trying to break out of your shell—not crawl back in and hide there all weekend.

Instead, rent something that gives you a good chuckle; something immature, goofy, politically incorrect, or even downright bawdy. As a result you will sleep better, bond with your movie-watching companions, and you will find yourself re-energized by the time you wake up the next morning.

Don't take my word for it; re-read the first few quotes in this section.

It's scientific!

Note to Self:

This release of adrenalin and endorphins caused by laughter does two things for us physically. First, we get energized from a good laugh and, second, we tend to relax after a good laugh with a sigh.

The irony of laughter

"Everyone loves to laugh." What's so funny about this truism is that *most of us don't. Discovery Health* claims, "By the time a child reaches nursery school, he or she will laugh about 300 times a day. Adults laugh an average of 17 times a day."

Worse yet, those in the majority of non-laughers also judge those who *do* laugh a lot. Think about it: some of your co-workers are laughing over in a corner of the office, what do you think about them? "Hmm—they're not working very hard," "Slackers," "Now, that's not very professional" and, if you are a woman, you're thinking, "I'll bet they are talking about me!"

As we have seen in the last few sections, the research on laughter in our lives shows us that, hands down, laughter not only energizes us, but it helps prevent depression, relieves pain, makes us more creative, and gets us to work earlier— and we stay longer. We are more creative and less stressed, so we tend to be better problem solvers.

We are healthier because we are laughing, and when we are healthier we tend to take fewer days off due to illness or straight fatigue. Also, because we are healthier we tend to look better, and when we look better we tend to like ourselves more, and when we like ourselves more we tend to give better service to others.

Because we like ourselves more we tend to be better lovers, and according to a 2003 German survey, when we are better lovers, we tend to "fool around" more often and researchers claim that people who fool around the most are supposed to be the most intelligent!

So it's a *win, win, win, win, win*!

Do you need more convincing?

Note to Self:

The research on laughter in our lives shows us that, hands down, laughter not only energizes us, but it helps prevent depression, relieves pain, makes us more creative and gets us to work earlier—and we stay there longer.

Step 2
Start by Laughing at Yourself

When my daughter Chloe was only five years old, she was helping me pack one day for yet another trip. She was choosing the clothes as fast as I was realizing everything she chose no longer fit me. Then it hit me! I said, "Chloe, I'm going to show you a dress you've never seen." From the back of the closet I pulled out that dress that definitely doesn't fit—the ole wedding dress.

Now, Chloe had never been to a wedding in her life and I realized in that moment that no matter what you look like, smell like, or what you might have screwed up that day, if your kids are under 12 or over 25 you are the king or queen of the world to them. She said to me, "Mom, it's just like Cinderella. Try it on!"

So I pulled and squeezed myself into this 80s mermaid style wedding dress, three sizes too small, and stood there in front of this wide-eyed little girl, and she proclaimed, "Mom, you are beautiful!"

At which point I swung around and pointed out that the zipper was ten inches away from being able to be done up. (Because, of course, I'm adult and by this point an official expert in finding the negative).

Now, if I had been a smart mom that day, I would have just stayed up in the bedroom and laughed with her but off I went downstairs to show my husband. As Kevin sat on the couch doing the "clicker thing" and biding his time, I knew that he was thinking to himself, "What do I say? What do I say?"

The first thing out of his mouth was, "Hey honey, do you think you'll ever fit in that dress again?"

"So where's the funny in all this?" you ask.

Well, as I was wallowing in my own self pity because I no longer fit in my wedding dress, mad at my husband for asking the obvious question, I moped my way down to the TV that night and found myself watching a documentary on the damage that Hurricane Andrew had left in Miami that year. (Talk about a mood swing.)

I got the message pretty quick and said a little thank you for the perspective kick in the butt that day. I guess the moral of this story is that being able to find the funny in situations involving ourselves is one of the best coping mechanisms we can nurture.

After all, we never know when it might come in handy.

Note to Self:

Pack "the dress" away, so you don't have to look at it every time you go into your closet.

Simple Shift #4
Life's Ultimate Goal
Aim to be Happy

Whether you are consciously aware of it or not, we humans are continually pursuing those things we call happiness, contentment, inner peace, or just a stronger sense of meaning in our lives. It doesn't matter whether we're planning a vacation, getting up the nerve to ask that special someone in accounting out on a date, working up our nerve to ask for a raise, starting an exercise program, or starting a savings plan, we are all—constantly—on the eternal quest for *happiness*.

I don't know how many of us actually find it, but what I *have* come to understand is that it takes *tons* of energy to get "there." And we don't actually ever "get there" because we actually bring happiness with us. That's right: You already have everything in you to realize your own happiness right now.

Remember that perspective shift we talked about a few sections back: choose happiness and your journey is mostly over—the destination is right in front of you, if you'll only reach out and take it. The problem with most of us, I've realized, is that the closer we get to happiness the more we fear it.

It's like we've built it up to this huge ball of fire in our minds, and the minute we're close enough to touch it we're afraid we might get burned. I have also come to realize that each of us defines this thing we call happiness in a very different way.

For some it's good health, good friends, a job well done, good food, a home that welcomes you at the end of the day, healthy kids, a great boat, vacations to warm destinations, your membership at the Club—I could go on and on and still never get to the end of this literally endless list.

Whatever happiness means to you, it is truly just relative to *you*. Remember, we bring it with us. Start carrying yours around today.

Note to Self:

You already have everything in you to realize your own happiness right now.

Step 1
Create Your Own Recipe
for Happiness

Too often we wait around for others to define our happiness—or even "bring" us happiness, like the pizza guy showing up at the door. I say "phooey." Design your own recipe: what brings you joy? Where do you hang your soul when you are stressed?

Start paying attention to these answers. Actively seek out the things that make you happy; weed out the things that make you unhappy. It is literally like a recipe for happiness: you add the ingredients you want and take out those that cause bitterness and other nasty tastes.

Begin gathering the ingredients that bring joy to your life and mix them together more actively and *a lot* more often. I can't give you the recipe; you have to create it on your own. You have to isolate the ingredients, mix them in the proper proportion, use them when necessary, and save some for later.

The best part is, as I said earlier, we don't "find" happiness we just "rediscover" it. Happiness is inside us; always has been and always will be. We just need to scrape off the layers of stress, worry, fear, guilt, shame, pride, ego, and other junk to get back to it.

Note to Self:

You already have everything in you to realize your own happiness right now.

Simple Shift #5
Life's Ultimate Skill
Shifting Perspectives

Whether it's about our children, our spouse, our job, our home, our health, or our weight, we view the world from our own perspective. It's our point of view, our outlook on life, a constant, 24/7 feeling that colours how we act, talk, look, and even feel.

We often live for years, decades even, without a major shift in our perspective. From time to time, however, our perspective gets kicked right in the butt. For many people, the terrorist attacks on New York and Washington on September 11, 2001 were the first real, major wake-up call, the first drastic shift in how we perceive our lives.

Those events changed how we viewed the world. We saw people on our street differently; we hugged our kids harder. I recall hearing media experts who thought it would be a lifetime shift, but it lasted only 60 days.

People acted different, attended church, stayed away from Vegas; mental health issues increased, Disney vacations dropped—and then the effect wore off. Other disasters took precedence. In my town, Kelowna, BC, the fires of 2003 saw hundreds of homes burn and more in danger, thousands of people evacuated, and the entire community shifted. The 2004 tsunami and 2005 hurricane saw shifts lasting a few weeks. We shifted into caring mode, then as we saw water being pumped out and the lights turned back on, it was less than two weeks of shift.

Do you see a pattern? Perspective shifts are like yo-yo diets; we lose weight or care for a while, and then it's right back to square one. Often we grow harder after we bounce back from the perspective shift than we were before.

Think of how the compassion for the victims of the tsunami and hurricane gave way to cynicism and doubt about how governments care for, plan for, and protect their people.

Perspective-shifting is our responsibility—it is our job to see that every day is a joy; we shouldn't have to wait for disasters—financial, natural, personal or otherwise—before we appreciate the life we live.

Think of how much joy there is to be had in life. Yes, there are tough times for everyone, but is that any reason to give up and give over to negativity and doubt? Shifting perspective does not mean you discount anything you are currently going through. It does mean, however, that you do just that: shift your perspective. Consider the situation, look at it with an open mind, and put it in perspective as part of a larger picture.

If you're tired of world hunger, do something about it. Donate some money or drop off canned goods or volunteer at a food bank. If you want to stop feeling victimized take positivity training or learn self-defense; if you want to help others become an advocate or volunteer at a battered woman's shelter.

The point is you have a choice; remain bummed out and apathetic or take action and shift your perspective to the positive. You see, it's the Shift part that requires movement. Move on something and see how your sights shift, too. You don't have to save the entire world to be happy; sometimes just saving your little corner of the world has a ripple effect that shifts not only your perspective, but those who come in contact with you every day.

You can not only *feel* the change, you can *be* the change....

Note to Self:

Answer this question, "What's one wonderful thing that's happened to me already today?" Be grateful for the large and small things in your everyday life.

26 instant perspective-shifting words

I know life takes over; it's hard to appreciate the beauty, joy, and sunshine of every day when you're facing back-to-back deadlines before you even get out of bed in the morning. But as our teachers used to say, "you're only cheating yourself" if you let the beast get the best of you and skip out on all the joy a great perspective-shift has to offer. To help you in this goal, here are my top 26 favourite perspective-shifting words. Try one today; I promise you'll love it:

1. Joy
2. Laughter
3. Fun
4. Appreciation
5. Gratitude
6. Delight
7. Excitement
8. Happiness
9. Bliss
10. Ecstasy
11. Exhilaration
12. Rapture
13. Thrill
14. Holiday
15. Vacation
16. Love
17. Lust
18. Desire
19. Buzz
20. Kick
21. Risk
22. Adventure
23. Quest
24. Journey
25. Possibility
26. Create

Note to Self:

You're only cheating yourself if you let the beast get the best of you and skip out on all the joy a great perspective-shift has to offer.

Simple Shift #6

Live the Shape You're In
Get Comfortable in Your Own Skin

What shape are you in? I know this isn't a diet book, and that's why I mean that literally: what "shape" are you in? My guess is that, like me, you are about 35-ish. Maybe you are 25-ish, 45-ish, 55-ish, and maybe even 65-ish. But here's what I came to realize around 38-ish: This body I've been given… is what I have to work with. That's it!

It's a right of passage, I suppose, this giving up of the façade and facing what, who, and where we really are. Somewhere between 35 and 45 we wake up and look in the mirror and decide—"This is what I've got to work with"—and come to terms with it. Now it's finally time to spend our energies on the other things besides trying to mould ourselves into someone else.

We have to start getting comfortable in our own skin; after all, this is the skin we're in. We can't trade it in; we can only renovate. So whether you are tall, short, thin, chubby, blonde, gray, brown, or bald—this is it. Get used to it.

You see, throughout our lives we spend tons of energy trying to be something we're not. But if you are truly going after the ultimate goal of happiness, you must get over yourself.

So let's take a look at how similar—and how different— we really are by examining the four basic types of human personalities. Now I have combined a few descriptions of personalities here, but they all really do come down to the basic four styles. You are either Structured/ Driver, Thinker/ Analyzer, Promoter/ Socializer, or a Supporter/ Relator.

One of my favourite sayings from *Guilt-Free Accountability*, a book I co-wrote, is, "Don't be Cranky, be a BAG! Bold, Adventurous, and Gutsy." The following is a combination of these surveys. Here are the rules: choose a symbol, description, or BAG type that appeals to you more than any of the others. You may like a couple, you may even like three. I've never met anyone who likes all four and if you are sitting there saying to yourself, "Hmm, I don't like any of them!" Well, let me just tell you that you are a "triangle."

1. **Box**   **The Driver**   **Flight Bag**
2. **Triangle** **The Thinker**   **Computer Bag**
3. **Squiggle** **The Socializer** **Sports Bag**
4. **Circle**   **The Relater**   **Gift Bag**

The Shapes Test has been around for years. Dr. Susan Dellinger developed a program similar to this in 1978, that still to this day provides people with loads of insights into themselves. Who would think that shapes would be so "on the mark" that it's frighteningly funny and predictable. Before we begin, here is a quick chart showing the indicative characteristics of each shape:

Open
(relationship oriented)

The Relator (circle)

- Relationship oriented but slower, more indirect
- Good listener
- Good people skills
- Fear of not being included
- Well suited to working in Human Resources
- Steady
- Likes to spend time getting to know others
- Doesn't like conflict
- Available for others to "cry on their shoulder"
- Decorates with lots of pictures, candles, dried flowers
- Stressed by pushy behaviour

The Socializer (squiggle)

- Open to relationships (sometimes too open)
- Loves the spotlight, high energy, dynamic
- Interactive
- Persuasive
- Great energy at the beginning of projects
- Easily bored
- Not good at working alone
- Lack follow-through
- Needs to be made accountable
- Impatient
- Loves "the big picture"
- Doesn't buy cars—Squiggles wear them!
- Motto—"Here for a good time, not a long time"

Indirect
(slow-paced)

Direct
(fast-paced)

The Thinker (triangle)

- Self-contained and stays focused on tasks
- Strong attention to detail, analytical
- Likes processes; asks "how does that work"
- Very accurate, cautious
- Great follow-through—Thinkers finish projects started by Socializers
- Likes to work independently
- Suffers "paralysis by analysis"
- Procrastinates for fear of making mistakes
- Take lots of pride in their work
- Double-checks; measures twice, cuts once
- Stresses over surprises, mistakes, and last minute changes
- Needs to work on "change readiness skills"

The Director (square)

- Fast-paced and task-oriented
- In control and in charge
- Gets things done by telling, not asking
- Steps on toes but doesn't realize it
- Motivated by results and "bottom line"
- Dominant
- Poor listener
- Stressed by time wasters
- Motto: "When I want your opinion, I'll give it to you"

Self-contained
(task oriented)

Box:
AKA Drivers/Controllers/Flight BAGS

These folks like structure. They like everything in its place and everything has a place. They like making their decisions based on information and they make them fast. They do not like talking about personal stuff at work and really don't feel it belongs there. Their biggest fear is being out of control—or at least appearing to be out of control. They are great visionaries and can lead and push their teams to do their best. In most crowds, they make up less than 1% of the population, but they wish everyone was more like them. Structured and well organized.

Triangle:
AKA Thinkers/Analyzers/ Computer BAGS

Because this symbol is found most often in math, those who like to "figure things out" are attracted to this shape. They are great researchers, very resourceful, and love gathering information. I always like to say that information gathering to them is an erotic experience as they tend to gather, and gather, and gather, info.

Triangles coupon clip and, more than likely, have a coupon wallet organizer. They cost compare and even figure out how much gas they will use if they drive to one store or another to make that purchase they have pondered for a few months. Triangles tend to not believe anything until someone gets them some stats, preferably accompanied by a graph.

Their biggest fear is making a mistake, so they will do and redo and redo. They base their decisions on information but they like making decisions slowly, just to make sure they don't make those mistakes. In most crowds, triangles make up about 3-5% of the population.

Squiggles:
AKA Socializers/Promoters/ Sports BAGS

These folks are here for a good time, not a long time. Everything to them is a window of opportunity: fun, fun, fun. That's their lifelong motto. They don't take "no" for an answer. In fact, they don't ask permission in the first place; they just do whatever they want and beg for forgiveness afterward. They also find themselves saying, "I've gotten by on personality this long, let's just see if I can push this one more day...." Their biggest fear is boredom. That and, of course, not being invited to the party. They have great energy and enthusiasm for almost everything, but lack the discipline to follow up and focus. If this is you, just sit and think for a moment about how you do your housework. Scary, isn't it? Squiggles make decisions based on emotion and they make them fast. This group makes up the majority of the population—about 75%.

Circles:
AKA Relaters/Supporters/ Gift BAGS

I always say I should start with these folks as their biggest fear is not being included. They are the best communicators because they actually listen, because they really do care about the rest of us. They do wear their hearts on their sleeves and can tell with a quick glance at their calendars whose birthday, anniversary, or retirement is coming up as they have all this info documented in their Daytimers. You can peg these folks as there is just something about their look that says,

"Hug me." They usually have dried flowers in their offices, candy dishes, and pictures of all their kids, their kids' kids and, of course, every pet they've ever had. They have a tough time with the word "no" and, whenever they say it, they feel *guilt*. As a group, they make up about 20% of the population.

What you can expect from your BAG personalities

Working with the Computer BAG (Thinker, Analyzer)

Action orientation:	Requires time and uses information
Psychological need:	Security
Values in others:	Facts, knowledge, and rationale
Dislikes:	Hype

In the group, you might expect that they...
* Follow a logical process and prefer to stay on track with agendas
* Do not like to be rushed...allow them to take the time they need
* Want claims backed up with evidence, facts, and figures—avoid gimmicks!

Working with the Flight BAG (Driver, Director, Controller)

Action orientation:	Decides quickly and uses information
Psychological need:	Control of self and circumstances
Values in others:	Stick to business
Dislikes:	Being manipulated

In the group, you might expect that they…
- Need a clear, concise overview prior to going into detail
- Need alternative choices to allow the "Flight BAG" to retain a feeling of control
- Need to see end results, overall results, and completion of goals quickly
- Are impatient with unnecessary details

Working with the Sports BAG (Socializer, Promoter)

Action orientation: Decides quickly and uses feelings
Psychological need: Status and attention
Values in others: Enthusiasm and energy
Dislikes: Embarrassment and laziness

In the group, you might expect that they…
- Need fast-paced process or you might "lose" them
- Want meetings to be kept on track
- The "Sports BAG" will tend to get off topic and should subtly be led back to the topic
- Values process in terms of fun, energy, and status

Working with the Gift BAG (Supporter/ Relater)

Action orientation: Requires time and uses feelings
Psychological need: Association
Values in others: Sincerity
Dislikes: Being left out

In the group, you might expect that they…
- Need to break the ice with a personal comment
- Appreciate a sincere interest in them as individuals and

have a need for common ground
- Like to see an emphasis on family and/ or "emotional health" of organization
- Don't respond well to high pressure
- Prefer not to argue—they require harmony

So, how'd you do? If you knew right away who you were, great; it will take far less time to drop the façade and get on with living the shape you're in. If you are still waffling between this shape and another, I don't know what to tell you.

Here's what I do know: You have always known who you are and what your basic style has been. For some reason, it takes us some living to come to grips with the fact that we don't change as we age, and if you are like most of us, truly going after that ultimate goal of "Happiness," then get over yourself and start just being you, more often.

Save your energy for the cold days. Don't get me wrong; all of us wear different shapes at different times in our lives. We carry different BAGS depending on what's happening at that time. We get along with some folks more than others; that's just the way it is. But if you are yourself more often than not, you will know how to be more effective with all kinds of folks, whether that's at work, at home, or in your community. Get comfortable in your own skin—it takes too much energy to keep on the mask. Deepak Chopra says, "Our greatest purpose is to be ourselves."

As I like to say, "The rest is just details."

Note to Self:

It's a right of passage, I suppose, this giving up of the façade and facing what, who, and where we really are.

Perfectly "priceless" perspectives

Remember the MasterCard commercial that said, "Haircut, $29; spa treatment, $72; manicure, $30; tickets to your ten-year reunion, $50; the look on your ex-boyfriend's face: priceless?"

Well, I have my own "priceless" version of that now-famous commercial. It has a lot to say about living the shape you're in with no regrets and all kinds of laughs. I was to speak in Vancouver and, as luck would have it, I had the flu. Not just that, but I had mistakenly assumed—must have been the DayQuil—that four hours with the girls in the back of the van would help us "bond."

But wait, it gets better: My old high school girlfriend had graciously offered us two of her spare rooms where we would be spending the night. So as we approached her house, I naturally called to let her know we were nearly there when she said the immortal line, "Guess who's coming to dinner?" Turned out it was *my* ex-boyfriend, a man I hadn't seen in a dozen or more years.

So here was *my* new version of the famous commercial: "The bra I wish I had put on, the hair that wasn't washed, the makeup that wasn't applied, and let's face it, the thirty-five pounds I'd put on since the last time he saw me... the look on my ex-boyfriend's face? Oh, total relief!"

And for everything else, there's Scotch!

Seriously, though, you can't sweat the small stuff—it shouldn't even make you blush! Because the small stuff happens all the time, every day. We can't live in fear of running into this old chum when we haven't washed our hair or that co-worker when we're having that extra glass of wine—we'd never leave the house!

Put your life in perspective—and take it back from the

worry, the fear, and the keeping up with the Joneses, the Smiths, and everybody else we're so busy trying to impress. I say impress yourself first; the rest will fall into place.

Note to Self:

We often worry too much about what others think about us, when they are usually not thinking about you at all.

Are you a better parent in public than you are in private?

Let's face it, we all have public and private personas. (If you think you're immune, just ask your spouse or your kids.) It's almost second nature to wear as many masks out of doors as we take off behind them. We have the stern mask we use for telemarketers, one we'd never use on family and friends. We have our supplicating "employee" mask, our sickeningly sweet "old person" mask, our semi-fake "just ran into an old acquaintance in the frozen foods aisle" mask and, last but not least, our plastered on "holiday" mask.

All of which begs the questions, "Are you a better parent in public? Has the darker side of yourself reared its nasty head since you've had kids? Does your public 'I love my kids' mask go on when you leave the house—and come right back off once you're safe inside? What is it with that?"

I was a much better parent before I had children. (Did I just say that?) I had the best ideas on how to raise them, what I'd never do, say, or feel! Then reality hit, and I ended up sounding just like all those people I swore I'd never sound like.

I love my kids. We all love our kids. We'd do anything for them, spend any amount of time, money, energy, blood, sweat or tears to see them succeed. So why is it all the meltdowns seem to happen with our kids?

I seldom work in my own town; most of the time I am on the road, talking to people just like you. But I was actually working in my own city recently, so I did the usual morning routine: get up, get the kids up, make breakfast, get them dressed, hair, teeth, lunches, find their homework, book orders, library returns, sign this and that form. Oh yeah, and get myself done up (now that threw a wrench in my normal routine).

So to say I was on the whirlwind is putting it mildly. My daughter Chloe, who is 13 this year, said as we were flying out the door, "Mom, are you always this cranky before you go off to be motivational?"

Ouch, the truth hurts.

Note to Self:

I was a much better parent before I had children.

Simple Shift #7
Life's Second Ultimate Goal
The Fewest Regrets Possible

Did I say that "happiness" was life's ultimate goal? Whoops! Actually, there are two ultimate goals in life. Yes, the first is happiness and the second is this: when eventually we leave the world, we want to do it with the fewest regrets possible. So, to recap:

- **Life's Ultimate Goal # 1:** *happiness*
- **Life's Ultimate Goal # 2:** *the fewest regrets possible*

I have spoken to several nurses who work with aging patients and they all confirm the same message: their patients are never embarrassed or regretful over things *they have done in their lives*. But they all regret the things *they never did*.

So with all this said, where do we start?

Start by letting yourself off the hook. Seriously, frankly who cares if you are not great at something? Will the world stop moving? Will the mountains topple? Will your street implode? Hardly. Life will go on whether you are great at something or just merely have fun trying. Just start something. Move on anything and see where it takes you.

It is good to try new things.

My point is: don't regret the things you've done that failed or didn't live up to your expectations. So you didn't get that job promotion; so you acted up at the office Christmas party; so you didn't have a 4.0 GPA in college. Get over it and move on.

Regrets are like worries; they're useless, with quick expiration dates. The crazy thing is, intellectually speaking, we all know perfection doesn't even exist, but for some strange reason we've bought into the idea that it's worth going after. Here's what I have found out about doing the things you want to really try: it's never about what you think it's about.

For instance, taking that great new job is often fantastic— but not for the reasons you at first thought it would be. Moving into that new house turns out to be great, but not because of the features you drooled over when you were house hunting. The blind date you were so worried about didn't turn out like you planned—it turned out even better!

The great thing about unexpected joys is that you don't find any of them until you are in the middle of the experience. Trust yourself enough to take risks anyway. You will be pleasantly surprised and, best of all, you won't even think about *regrets*.

Note to Self:

I have spoken to several nurses who work with aging patients and they all confirm the same message: their patients are never embarrassed or regretful over things they have done in their lives. *But they all regret the things* they never did.

"Perfectionism" is a Disease We Just Have to Get Over

If you are one of those eternally unhappy people who is constantly in pursuit of perfection, I have good news for you: it does not exist. Now, don't get me wrong: I do believe in *excellence*. I know we can all do more—and better—than we are doing now.

After all, the stats on human potential are mind-blowing: we use only about 10% of our brains in the first place. The difference is this: when a perfectionist does the best job they could possibly have done, they are *still* not satisfied!

Now, there are two kinds of perfectionists: the first type are people who have a high standard for themselves; the second have high standards for themselves—and everyone else.

If you are the second type, the bad news is you are going to go through life constantly being disappointed, because the "rest" of us are going to keep making mistakes and letting you down.

But, I have some great advice for you, no matter which type of perfectionist you are. By the end of our time together on these pages, you won't be perfect, but you'll feel a whole lot better about your, my, and just about everybody else's imperfections.

Note to Self:

When perfectionists do the best job they could have possibly done, they are still *not satisfied!*

Pushing past perfection — the Towel Test

Before you attempt what I call the "Towel Test," keep in mind that everything we try to change in our lives takes practice. If we could all just wake up tomorrow, happy and perfect, nobody would need this book—or any self-help book, for that matter.

For all you perfectionists and perfectionists-in-training out there, however, here's some homework: tomorrow, when you get out of the shower, don't hang your towel on the towel bar nice and tidy like you do every day.

Instead, throw that wet towel on the floor and march out of the bathroom. Yes, that is what I said, throw it down, wet and sloppy, and just storm off. Yes, yes, I know, you will experience some slight heart palpitations, but persevere.

Leave your house, go to work, and try to concentrate on the day's tasks. At the end of the day when you walk in your front door, you will discover life's most sublime joy: "Wow, I am still alive."

Okay, sure, I am poking some fun here, but the towels are a great place to start. After all, no one will be hurt if you start with towels. The purpose of doing this seemingly impossible task is to just see how you feel being "out of control" for a few short hours. Tell yourself you are "putting it in perspective." You see, it doesn't matter if you care or don't care about how straight your towels hang on the towel bar. It doesn't matter if you're bugged because you didn't get your bed made or because some dishes went unwashed. Leave the scrubby out of the little frog's mouth for once. And heaven forbid, that you get a bit miffed that one of your friends or family members show up at your door without calling first cause you didn't have time to *get yourself together…. But*, if you are spending energy on all this kind of stuff, then we need to sit down and have a little one-on-one chat. So don't pass go, don't collect your perfect two one-hundred-dollar bills. *No!* Go straight to "You Need a Life" Railway Company, just next to the "I can't afford anything near the Boardwalk property," and sign up for the Towel Test.

Note to Self:

Keep in mind that changing things in life takes practice.

Perfection is painful for you and everyone else around you…

The pursuit of perfection is exhausting, alienating, lonely, non-fulfilling, and just not healthy. You can't reach your ultimate goal in life—happiness— by pursuing perfection. That's because the main problem with pursuing perfection is that it gives us the ultimate "out." It secretly makes us feel better to have an unattainable goal. That way, when we can't attain it, it makes all of our other, more attainable, goals feel okay if we fail them as well.

To make it simple: if you still buy into the idea, "if you can't do it well, don't do it at all," then you will not become who you are supposed to become. You will never be happy because what's the point of anything?

The point is not perfection, only excellence. You see, I do believe in excellence. In fact, I have often been asked the difference between perfection and excellence. The difference is this: when you have done your absolute best, no matter what the result, that's excellence. A perfectionist doesn't see this: a perfectionist sees only what remains undone, and it eats them up inside.

On the other hand, someone who recognizes and respects their continual quest for excellence understands that they've done the absolute best they could possibly do on any given task, considering whatever is on their plate at that time, so they actually lay their head down at night and breathe a sigh of satisfaction. It doesn't eat them up inside, only lets them get a good night's rest so they can get up and fight the good fight the next day!

Motivation comes from movement

Motivation does not come from someone talking at you, or from listening to a CD. Motivation comes from movement: it's a physics thing. It is literally about putting one foot in front of another and moving towards something—a goal, a desire, a dream you want to experience.

Just get started and let inertia, sometimes called the snowball effect, move you along. You will go for a while and you might slow down, but it will pick up again. I call this *Motivational Movement*™. The key here is to let go of the outcome as so many of us are tied to what it should look like. I honestly believe, who cares what it looks like? No goal is ever about what you think it's going to be about anyways. So just get started and see where it takes you. And that, my dear perfectionists, is the ultimate goal for you in this book: *Just get started.*

Simple Tip for Getting Started

Don't think! Our heads often get in the way of our acting on stuff, so you need to use the "don't think!" method of getting started. Let's say you want to go for a walk. But it's a bit chilly outside and your head kicks in. You simply say to yourself, "don't think, don't think, don't think!" You say this as you are tying your shoes and as you head out the door. So use the "don't think" method of getting started.

Note to Self:

Jot down some of your goals, move on them, and see where they take you. Just notice how your physical energy picks up.

Simple Shift #8
Allow Less Latitude on Your Attitude

Not to sound too much like a greeting card, but I like to say that "Attitude is a gift you give yourself." Attitude is not dependent on the weather, your bank account, your social status, your rank at work, or even your love life—attitude starts with *you*.

What is your attitude?

Is it good or bad?

How do you see life?

Overwhelmingly positive or downright depressing?

If you're already making up excuses or rationalizing away your answer, my guess is that your attitude is not so hot! I think attitude is important enough to give a name to, and so when I speak of attitude it's not with a lowercase "a" but a capital one, as in Attitude Factor. That is because your Attitude truly *is* a factor in just about everything you do.

The bottom line is that attitude plays a *huge* part in who we are, what we do, and how we treat people along the way. Attitude has been linked with many extremes: from longevity to a shorter lifespan, from happiness to depression, from a healthy weight to obesity, and from low blood pressure to high.

Simple Shifts are designed not just to help you identify your attitude, but to keep it in check along the way. The third section of this book is entitled "When was the *last* time you did something for the *first* time?" For many of us, having a positive attitude is doing something for the first time.

Let's just hope after reading this Simple Shift, it won't be your last time…

Note to Self:

The bottom line is that attitude plays a huge *part in who we are, what we do, and how we treat people along the way.*

What is the Attitude Factor?

Your attitude is a factor in everything you do; that's why I call it the Attitude Factor. It is the muscle that binds the skeleton of your days together, the glue that holds your personality in place.

So what *is* the Attitude Factor? The Attitude Factor says that no equation ever evens out if you forget to *factor* in your *attitude.* In other words, we can't allow ourselves to be negative people any longer. The costs are just too high.

Think about how much energy you waste being down, depressed, sad, worried, doubtful, upset, wary, and just plain negative. Think about the opportunities you've missed to make new friends, court new business or close new deals because your two operating modes are "down and downer."

Note to Self:

Your attitude is a factor in everything you do. It is the muscle that binds the skeleton of your days together, the glue that holds your personality in place.

Take the Attitude Aptitude Test

Don't worry; it's not really a test. I won't grade you and the busybody reading this over your shoulder won't be able to quietly judge your score. The Attitude Aptitude Test is really just a guide to steer you through identifying a few of the easier ways to help adjust your attitude. It consists of one quick question—to be answered just as quickly—and an easy scale by which to judge your response. Ready? Okay, here goes:

1. Quick—don't over-think it, don't guess what the answer might mean—what is your first thought every new day?

If your first thought is positive, upbeat, and hopeful—congratulations! You have a great attitude. If you're like the majority in the world, however, and your thoughts are doom, gloom, woe, agony, and despair—you are working with a negative attitude—and at only about half of your capacity.

So, now you know one way or another: either you have a positive attitude (doubtful) or a negative one (more than likely). The only question that remains is, "What do you intend to do about it?"

Note to Self:

Remember your attitude (the way you see your life) affects how you experience your life.

Success Rule #2
Make positivity your default attitude:
Your three-step plan for a more
positive attitude—every day

We all have a default setting, that "mode" we wake up in and, for the most part, stick with all day. This section is about making positivity your default attitude. We've already discussed how important the Attitude Factor is, and even determined which side of the equation you come down on: positive or negative.

Now it's time to do something about it. The following three steps will help you make positivity your default attitude—but only if you let them:

1. Make it a habit

You know what I love about habits? They're self-created and ultimately reversible. That's right: the bad habits you live with, including seeing the gray skies before the blue, are all self-created, but the good news is that you can turn them around!

We create the habit of negativity by practicing it, over and over and over again. When every thought is, "There's no way this is going to happen for me" or "This will end in tears" or "I guarantee I won't get that promotion," you are actively creating a habit of negative thoughts. And remember, what you focus on *expands*. So the more negativity you see, the more negativity you experience, and as you experience more negativity, this only proves to you how negative it all really is. This is how it expands to become your primary experience and view of your life and the world. Sometimes this has been called a "self-fulfilling prophecy."

Break the habit by replacing every negative thought with a positive one. This is not just some bumper sticker; it works! You have to be conscious about it, though. Habits can be reversed but it takes work. You have to actively think positive. And you know what? It's catchy. The more positive things you think, the more they happen. You just need to catch yourself when negative thoughts come in. Recognize them, and if you can, replace them.

It's not quite as simple as wishing up a rainbow and following it to your own little pot of gold, but it works along the same basic principle. How? Well, every positive thought is like that proverbial rainbow; it may not lead to a literal pot of gold, but positive thoughts do have the power to change our brain chemistry. Endorphins are released when we think about positive things, which results in creating not only a healthier outlook, but also a healthier mind and body. Just remember this takes practice so be gentle on yourself as you start this change.

2. Practice Makes Improvement

Creating new habits or undoing old ones takes practice—and lots of it! Start small by shaking off your first negative thought of the morning and replacing it with a positive one. Just one, each morning. Then add another positive thought the next day, say maybe during rush hour. Then, the next day, in addition to your first positive thought of the morning and your second positive thought of the commute, add a third positive thought, maybe as you're pulling into the parking garage at work. Here is what these positive thoughts might sound like: just notice what you notice about yourself.

First positive thought of the morning: Instead of something negative like, "God, I don't want to go to work today," think of something positive like, "I really enjoy chatting with Cathy at coffee break."

Second positive thought of the morning: Instead of something negative during your commute like, "Why can't this jerk in the blue mini-van get in the right lane," think of something positive like, "After work I should go to the bookstore and get one of those self-help audio-books for the drive home…"

Third positive thought of the morning: Instead of something negative as you pull into the parking garage at work like, "Why is there never a space close to my office?" think of something positive like, "By parking farther away, I can walk longer and burn more calories…"

And so on…

Remember, it's easy to get discouraged—but by staying positive the habit gets easier over time. That's because the positive thoughts are like lifting weights; the more you do them, the stronger you get.

3. Commit first, create later

There is one easy way to stop yourself from falling back into bad habits and that's to take the choice away. The great Canadian philosopher Red Green (aka Steve Smith) once said in an interview, "Thank God we only live one hundred years. As people we procrastinate far too much already: if we had more time, we'd get nothing done!" The truth is that 99% of the population procrastinates, creating all sorts of reasons not to get going on things. I know that as a businesswoman that if I had created a program and gone out to try to sell it, I would never have started. So instead, I have always pushed my business forward using the strategy of selling the product or concept first. Then, I have been forced to create it. Whatever it is you want to move on, it does not have to be 100% done before you venture out to experience it.

This attitude approach takes some guts, and there is some risk but nothing in this crazy world was ever created with 100% of the research finished and every "i" dotted and "t" crossed. One note of caution here, however. This does not mean I think people should be stupid and not do some checking, just don't use the excuse that you haven't got all the information yet before you can move forward.

By leaping first over the fence of a positive attitude before you look for all that could go wrong, you avoid the risk of returning to the negative. As I said earlier, a positive attitude is a habit. It is also a much more exciting way to lead your life. Like all habits, the more you do it, the more you do it. Make positivity your default attitude and you *will* be more positive. It's far from easy, but it's just that simple.

Note to Self:

We all have a default setting, that "mode" we wake up in and, for the most part, stick with all day.

Simple Shift #9
Nix the Negative in Your Life

Negativity is like a disease: it is easily spread from one person to another. Our only defence is to learn how to deal with negativity on a daily basis. How we do that is uniquely personal, but I know for a fact that laughter is an instant and guaranteed remedy.

As we saw back in "Simple Shift #3," the many benefits of laughter are well-documented and, by those who enjoy them, well-received. The problem for most of us is that laughter is accidental; we don't go out and actively court laughter, or attract it to ourselves, or even create it for ourselves.

We rely on our funny friends, a humorous waiter, an actor or comedienne, or simply life's funny moments—which are admittedly few and far between—to happen *to* us rather than making them happen *for* us.

That is what *Find Your Own Funny Faster* is all about: making laughter when there is none around. Like everything worthwhile in life, personal accountability is a big part of *Find Your Own Funny Faster*—in fact, it's the driving force behind the movement and, to be honest with you, this entire book.

Finding the funny, the quirky and the obscure is a little like having "opposite day;" it's taking your own negative responses—and those of others—and turning them completely upside down. It's literally looking at life from a different perspective, all in the name of finding more to be positive about in our lives.

For instance, let's say a co-worker rushes into your cubicle to announce, "Holy crap, someone made a huge goof on the bid for the Bows account and now our whole department has to work through the weekend so we don't lose it completely!"

Naturally, there are two ways to respond to this news: with negativity or positivity.

A negative person might say, "Oh great, there goes my weekend! Now I'll be stuck in this horrid cubicle rewriting ad copy for the next forty-eight hours solid."

A positive person might say something more like, "Yippee! No soccer games, laundry, dusting, vacuuming, or walking the dog for the next forty-eight hours. Bring it on, Mr. Bows!" Note to self: Have you sat through a weekend soccer tournament lately?

It may seem oversimplified to always look for the positive with humour and a smile, but so what? What are you losing by looking on the bright side? When was the last time negativity paid more dividends then positivity? For that matter, when was the last time you were able to worry during a good laugh? Look for funny signs on the road, stories in the paper, and make sure you notice the funny things that the children in your life say. Some of our best material comes from our kids.

Humour isn't just the best medicine—sometimes it's the only cure for what ails us. It's one of the best bridges to healing when we are hurting. I say, laugh it off and be done with it. But don't wait for someone else to make you laugh—take matters into your own hands and fine your own funny faster!

Note to Self:

Simply put, everyone loves to laugh. Just find your own funny faster.

There is energy in negativity, unfortunately

Have you ever noticed that it's just as easy to pick up on negativity as it is to feed on positivity? Think about that one for a minute. Let's say you're in a motivational seminar where the speaker or leader is very upbeat and positive. When you walk out of the room, you feel energized, enthusiastic, hopeful, and overwhelmingly positive.

There's a lot of energy in that.

Now let's try a different scenario, one in which you're gathered around the water cooler gossiping about what a jerk your boss is. One negative comment feeds on the next until the gossip mill is flying and your heart is racing.

There's a lot of energy in that.

In fact, I think if there were a device to measure such energy the readings would be just about equal for positive emotions as they are for those of the negative kind. And since, in this fast-paced world of crushing deadlines, admittedly jerky bosses, irate customers, teenagers, and traffic jams, it's a whole lot easier to be negative than it is to be positive. Which kind of energy do you think we are drawn to most?

That's right: the dark side of negativity. In fact, we have a tendency to "one-up" each other when it comes to negativity. If I have a headache, no doubt you have a migraine. If you stubbed your toe, I can show you this swell bruise on my calf. If it's 20 degrees where I live, it's got to be 20 below where you reside—and snowing to boot!

This leads us to the Martyr Matrix, where everybody is so busy one-upping everybody else in the downward spiral that we all become martyrs to our very own misery.

How do you know if you're a martyr?

Simply put, "You might be a martyr if... going to the bathroom with the door closed is considered pampering yourself."

Or, "You might be a martyr if... joining a 12-Step program is not appealing to you because there aren't enough steps."

Oh—I have more.

Note to Self:

I think if there were a device to measure such energy, the readings would be just about equal for positive and negative emotions.

Simple Shift #10
Stress Resilience
How's That Working for You?

We each have our own personality style, but did you know that even our way of dealing with stress is unique to us? Over the years, having worked for, consulted with, and spoken to literally tens of thousands of willing participants in my ongoing personality experiments, I have identified four specific personality "stress" styles:

1. Perfects
2. Pleasers
3. Popeyes
4. Hurry-ups

It is as important to know how you deal with stress as it is to deal with it in the first place, and knowing which of the four types you are is a great start in handling stress the right way—your way:

Personality Stress Style # 1: Perfects

Perfects deal with stress as one might imagine: by ignoring it and acting as if everything is just perfect. Perfects would have been seen "rearranging deck chairs on the Titanic." While the house is burning around them they're watering the house plants instead of dousing the flames. Anything to continue the fiction that nothing is happening, nothing's going wrong—and everything's quite all right, thank you very much!

Ignoring stress is just as bad as reacting poorly to stress, in fact, it may be even worse. At least responding to stress poorly lets you acknowledge it; you may not get it all out but you get some of it out. By reacting as if stress isn't happening, you simply delay the reaction until, denial after denial, that pile of pushed down stress explodes and comes spilling out all over your life! Then what will the neighbours think?

Personality Stress Style # 2: Pleasers

Pleasers are close to Perfects in that they like order amidst the chaos. In this case, however, they add the double burden of not only seeking perfection when stress rears its ugly head, but also doing it at great cost to themselves. That is because their idea of perfection in the face of stress is pleasing others first and themselves second.

The worst thing about pleasers is that they take in not only the stress that happens to them, but also the stress of others as well. That makes them "stress collectors," gathering even more stress to add to their own. Pleasers seem to attract stress, perhaps because they are so eager to please that they will listen to anyone's sob story—even that of a complete stranger.

They do, however, have a stress release and that happens through passive-aggressive expression. In other words, they say "yes" until the proverbial pile is almost smothering them and then they blow. Meanwhile, everyone else around them looks on in astonishment, saying things like, "What? You never act like this! Honey, is something wrong?" And, of course, the Pleaser's patent answer is, "Oh no, nothing."

And, to top it off, they end up apologizing for not listening sooner...

Personality Stress Style # 3: Popeyes

Popeyes are close to Perfects, but they have one other redeeming quality. Not only do they like things done in a certain way, but (in the immortal words of that beloved cartoon sailor) their life motto is, "I am what I am." In other words, Popeyes think to themselves, "I *could* delegate this to someone, but they'll probably screw it up, so I'll just end up doing it over again. I might as well just do it myself and get it done faster the first time." What's really going on here is an underlying fear that if they delegate, and whoever takes on the task makes a mistake, it will reflect on them personally.

Some slightly reformed Popeyes have tried the "delegation thing" but then they hover like a helicopter over the poor person, watching every move they make. Popeyes have to learn to let go of the need to be in control all the time. Because if they don't, the consequences are just too great.

What Popeyes get is alienation, disgruntled team members and staff, lazy kids, and basically no clue about all the creativity that might exist in the folks around them. So, if you're a Popeye, here's your task to practice: Take a task, like getting your kids to clean up their room. Once they've done it, *do not* go back in and re-clean it. Sit on one hand and use the other one to cover your mouth, let the headache set in, and just see how uncomfortable you feel being out of control. Remember, in the end, this task really has *no* huge impact on the betterment of mankind.

If you are really brave, do the same task with a co-worker or staff person at work. No, don't get them to clean their room. Delegate something to them and *do not* hover. Just check in very occasionally. What you will find is you'll start to let go of some of your fears and your self perception will improve. And, gosh darnit, people will start to like you more.

Personality Stress Style # 4: Hurry-ups

Hurry-ups do just what their name implies; they respond to stress with speed. Unfortunately, they don't rush to relieve the stress—they only make it worse. Like Pleasers, Hurry-ups invite stress with their hectic pace. Speed can be helpful in situations where it is required, but stressful when that quick pace leads to sloppy mistakes or extra work.

Hurry-ups can improve how they handle stress by simply slowing down, deep breathing, and prioritizing. But, as the name implies, that is simply not in their nature and, in fact, going slower would make their lives *more* stressful, not less. (PS: You know you are a Hurry-up if you were impatient reading this paragraph and found out your style was last in the list of four!)

Note to Self:

The worst thing about Pleasers is that they take in not only the stress that happens to them, but others' stresses as well.

Finding your three Cs: developing a stress-resistant personality

As we all know, handling stress improperly—or ignoring it all together—can lead to The Big B, or Burnout. Naturally, burnout conjures up negative thoughts and emotions in most of us and especially in those of us who have experienced it.

If we are facing burnout, in order to get out of survival mode and take control, we need to change the messages we are sending to our brains. Everyone experiences stress every day. Some of us lead extremely stressful lives but experience stress as being not so bad. What are the skills required to be more stress resistant?

Recent studies have found that people with high levels of stress but low levels of illness share three characteristics. They are called the "three Cs":

1. **Control**: a sense of purpose and direction in life.
2. **Commitment:** to work, hobbies, social life, or family.
3. **Challenge:** seeing changes in life as normal and positive rather than as an irritant and a threat.

Society, on the other hand, also encourages us to value another set of "three Cs":

1. **Cash**: work as much and as hard as you can to be a success.
2. **Cars**: one must keep up with the neighbours.
3. **Closet Space**: the bigger the closet, the more stuff you have.

These two lists represent the classic struggle between the head and the heart, between integrity and lack of it, between acquiring the brass ring and keeping self-respect.

As always, the key to success is *balance*.

We can't avoid stress, but we can avoid burnout, and better yet, *we can learn to stay well*.

Note to Self:

Life is a pendulum that swings back and forth between our personal values and societal pressures.

Simple Shift #11

Wearing Your Heart on Your Sleeve is a Good Way to Put Your Foot in Your Mouth
The Benefits of Communicating Effectively

Communication is the key to leading a happier, more productive life. Think about it: wouldn't your life be simpler if you didn't have to worry about putting your foot in your mouth each time you unclenched your teeth to say something in the first place?

In "Simple Shift 10" we talked about stress, and few things cause stress like worrying about your communication skills. Public speaking, asking the boss for a raise, clearing the air with your spouse, even talking to your kids—these are all communication issues that spike the blood pressure and double the stress!

A lot of our communication problems start when we mix personality stress styles, such as Pleasers and Perfects, with wanting those second three Cs—cash, cars, and closet space—to come up with what I call the Martyr Matrix.

In the Martyr Matrix, conversations hold so much weight it's almost impossible to communicate. Basically, martyrs hold all their thoughts in, only to cause themselves mental and physical angst. All the while having an internal conversation where self-pity and resentment mix to create a very unhappy heart and upset tummy.

Note to Self:

Communication is key to leading a happier, healthier, more productive life.

Know yourself, understand others and communicate effectively

Having effective communication skills means more than simply reading personality styles, but also actually *working with them*. In "Simple Shift #6," I introduced you to the four main personality styles: the Analyzer/ Triangle/ Computer BAG; the Driver/ Box/ Flight BAG; the Socializer/ Squiggle/ Sports BAG; and the Relater/ Circle/ Gift BAG.

In this section I'll help you work and communicate with them more effectively:

Working with the Analyzer/ *Triangle*

- **Buying style:** requires time and uses information
- **Psychological need:** security
- **Expectation from you:** product knowledge
- **Dislikes:** hype

TIPS:
- Provide a complete and logically laid out presentation.
- Do not rush Analyzers; allow them to take the time they need.
- Back up your claims with evidence, facts, and figures— avoid gimmicks.

Working with the Driver/ *Box*

- **Buying style:** buys quickly and uses information
- **Psychological need:** control
- **Expectation from you:** stick to business
- **Dislikes:** being manipulated

TIPS:
- Give a clear, concise overview of the presentation prior to going into detail.
- Provide alternative choices to allow the Driver to retain a feeling of control.
- Tailor the information given to the end use, the overall result, and to the completion of goals resulting from the use of your product/service.
- Do not provide unnecessary detail.

Working with the Socializer/ *Squiggle*

- **Buying style:** buys quickly and uses feelings
- **Psychological need:** status
- **Expectation from you:** enthusiasm
- **Dislikes:** embarrassment

TIPS:
- Keep your energy level high, and the pace of your presentation moving quickly.
- Carefully keep the presentation on track. The Socializer will tend to get off the topic, and must be subtly led back to the subject of discussion.
- Emphasize the product or service in terms of results and status. Terms such as "state of the art" or "fastest available" will appeal.

Working with the Relater/ *Circle*

- **Buying style:** requires time and uses feelings
- **Psychological need:** association
- **Expectation from you:** sincerity
- **Dislikes:** being left out

TIPS:

- Break the ice with a personal comment.
- Show a sincere interest in Relaters as people; search for common ground.
- Emphasize the benefit to the Relater's company, family, or organization.
- Do not come on too strong, too quickly, or in a manner which would be perceived as pressuring a Relater.
- Do not debate or argue with the Relater.
- Spend plenty of time asking questions.
- Demonstrate that you have their best interests at heart.

Note to Self:

Having effective communication skills means more than simply reading personality styles, but also actually working with them.

SHIFT... OR GET OFF THE POT — 93

Assertiveness Exercise

Most people have a difficult time distinguishing between aggressive and assertive behaviour. When passive people begin to ask for our needs to be met, we feel as though we are being very aggressive. This is usually not the case. Instead, we have to learn the difference between being assertive—putting our needs on an equal level with others—and being aggressive—always putting our needs first.

To further your understanding of communication, try this Assertiveness Exercise:

1. Where on the assertiveness grid do you find yourself?
Passive   Assertive   Aggressive

2. Write down your honest opinions on the following:
a) Society's view of passive men
b) Society's view of passive women
c) Society's view of aggressive men
d) Society's view of aggressive women

Most women who want to be assertive will subconsciously undermine themselves because they don't want anyone to think they are a *B!#@H*. Here's the good and the bad news: even when you are assertive, most times it won't make others change their behaviour. So you are assertive to take care of your own needs. When you put your head on your own pillow at night, you will feel like you took care of yourself today. And that's it!

Assertiveness Formula

1. **Know yourself.** If you find it difficult to be assertive in the moment, give it some time, gather your thoughts, write points down if you need to, and then go back to the person you need to confront.
2. **Respect the other person's point of view.** This doesn't mean you need to like or agree with them—just understand that from their perspective, they're right, and from yours, you're right.
3. **Always use "I" statements.** For instance, "I feel _____ when _____ " and "What I need is _____." This can stop the other person's feeling defensive.
4. **Practice, practice, practice.** You don't always get the response you want, but you do take care of your needs, which decreases stress and increases your total well-being.

Note: You can write down the thoughts you want to share with another person and it's fine to read them if necessary. Nerves can make it hard to express ourselves effectively, so notes can help.

Note to Self:
The Best Assertiveness Tip Ever

When someone asks a favour of you, no matter what the circumstances, don't answer right away. Think carefully: consider if you can and/or want to take on the request. If you think, " Yes, I can do this," you will have less resentment attached to your "yes." If you come back with a "no" and a very long-winded reason why attached to the "no," you will also have less guilt attached to the "no."

The doldrums of martyrdom

It gets awfully boring in the Martyr Matrix. All that back and forth can get tiring, particularly when no real information is being exchanged, just minor details about the doom and gloom of our (apparently) dull and dreary lives.

The problem with being a martyr is that it gets in the way of true listening. You can't have true communication without true listening. Why are martyrs such bad listeners? It's because they're so busy waiting to one-up the person they're talking to that they can't really concentrate on what the other person is saying.

Think about most conversations you have. It has become culturally acceptable to one-up each other in the gloom and doom department. We have made it OK to be part of the "Ain't It Awful Club," the "Whine Your Way to Alienation Group," or perhaps the "Stitch and Bitch" in the coffee room. We try to outdo each other in these clubs for one of two reasons: either, "If I go lower than you, then perhaps I'll make you feel better," or "Maybe I'll get more sympathy or attention." It serves a need and our culture has become OK with this.

Test: For the next couple of days pay more attention to conversations around you, at work, at the store, at home. Notice how positive or negative they are and force yourself not to engage in negative talk.

This verbal one-upmanship isn't a conversation, it's a game, and both parties are losers because nothing actually gets said. As a professional speaker, I take my conversations very seriously, and while I've been known to inject a few conversations with a joke to lighten the mood, I can tell you that the Martyr Matrix will stop any effective communication dead.

"How?" you might ask. Well, since the conversation tango takes two, if one of them makes an honest effort, the other usually responds. Not always, mind you—this takes some practice—but good conversations, like good friends, mature with time and require a little cooperation on both sides.

If you'll notice, the same information gets bandied about—just in a friendlier, more mutually communicative way. We're not talking global shifts in how you communicate here, just minor improvements that, over time, create not only better listeners but also better communicators.

Note to Self:

The problem with being a martyr is that it gets in the way of true listening. And, as we all know, you can't have true communication without true listening.

Section 2:

Are You on the
Deferred Life Plan?

Overview
"Everybody's Working for the Weekend"

Did you know that the very popular 80s hit "Everybody's Working for the Weekend" by Loverboy is still, decades later, the number one song played on most radio stations across North America on Fridays at five pm. We watch the clock waiting for bell to ring and "we're free!" Life is full of all sorts of well-meant "plans." There are savings plans; there are fitness plans; there are dental plans, and then there is what I call "The Deferred Life Plan." The Deferred Life Plan is just like a savings plan—you deny yourself today in hopes of a better tomorrow—only, there is no great big payoff at the end.

I suppose it's natural that we start investing in The Deferred Life Plan early. After all, we're taught its value in kindergarten where we learn all kinds of Deferred Life Plan laws like "Be still," "Sit in alphabetical order," "Use your inside voice" and, my favourite, "Just hold it until recess!"

After that, we're pretty much *all* on the Deferred Life Plan—for life. But you and I know better; we have just spent an entire section learning the mental, physical, and emotional benefits of living louder and laughing harder, two steps that are definitely *not* on the Deferred Life Plan.

This section is all about living more and denying yourself less. No, it's not about maxing out your credit cards or drinking to excess or making a life's goal of dining at every all-you-can-eat buffet in a 200-mile radius. It's about giving yourself permission to live life in the moment. We all need those other plans—savings, fitness, and dental—but we've invested enough by now in the Deferred Life Plan for it to start paying off—without delay!

Note to Self:

The Deferred Life Plan is just like a savings plan—you deny yourself today in hopes of a better tomorrow—only, without the great big payoff at the end.

SIifT... or Get Off the Pot — 99

Stop working for the weekend!

Life is a series of broken promises we make to ourselves in hopes of reaching that "perfect" us. Don't believe me? Does this sound familiar? "When Friday comes, then I'll really let my hair down." Is this a pretty common statement around your office? You spend all week complaining about how quickly the weekend went, only to watch the clock and count the days until good old "TGIF" rolls around. Then, when Friday finally comes, there is the laundry to do, the dinner to make, the kids' artwork to rearrange on the fridge, and you're usually too pooped to pop.

How about this famous statement? "When I get out of school, then life will really be mine, and it will all be great." But, that's not quite right, either. After school, you can go to college or get a job, both of which require lots of hard work to get ahead.

So you say to yourself, "Well, then when I get out of college, I'll really have it together, and life will really be great." And right after that you end up saying, "OK, well, when I get that job and start making twenty grand, thirty grand, forty grand, or whatever that 'right amount' of money is, then life will *really* kick into gear."

Then we realize that we think we need someone to share our life with so we think once we get married, "Well, then I'll *really* feel fulfilled and then I'll *really* live happily ever after."

But wait, the two of you then figure, "If we just have a few kids, then we will really feel fulfilled." Then you start saying, "When those kids leave home... *then* we'll have lots of time to do all the things we've been putting off." Gradually, inevitably, fruitlessly, life becomes a series of "When I..." moments that never quite gel into those much-coveted but ever-elusive, "Ah, now I'm really satisfied…" moments.

"When I retire…"

"When I lose that thirty pounds…"

"When I get that raise…"

"When I buy that Winnebago…"

Your "when" is right now; tomorrow will be too late. I have one message for you: *This Is It!* Your life doesn't start once you have more money, have a nicer home, better friend-ships, a better car, a slimmer waist, or a more fulfilling job. I'll admit that it does seem easier with all those things, but if you refuse to get on with your life *until some of these things fall into place,* then you are not really living at all, you are simply on the Deferred Life Plan.

This very moment you are reading this passage is *it*! Now, I'm not saying this is as good as it gets. But it is *it*. What if you never again fit into a size-32 waist? What if a mid-price sedan is the best car you'll ever afford? What if your house is the family homestead—for good? Well, okay, so what if it is?

Choose to make it—*all* of it—the best that you can. For-get size 32 for now and focus on buying clothes that show off your best assets. Buy the best mid-priced sedan you can afford and drive it into the ground with pride. Paint the house or redecorate the living room or just buy some new throw pil-lows for a splash of dash!

Life does not have be dull and dreary "until." Until this, until that. Until what? Think of all the days we've wasted wishing away our todays on tomorrows. What if today you just spent enjoying the present and living in the moment? Make a decision to change your TGIF (Thank God It's Fri-day) to TGIA (Thank God I'm Alive).

That's the quickest way I know to get off The Deferred Life Plan.

Note to Self:

Change your TGIF (Thank God It's Friday) to TGIA (Thank God I'm Alive).

Simple Shift #12
Tips to Re-energize and Balance Yourself

I realize that it is arrogant of me to suggest that you do anything else when most of us are living lives so busy that we are chronically fatigued to the point of physical and mental exhaustion. In fact, statistics say that half of the population suffers from some sort of insomnia or sleep deprivation.

And now I'm asking you to add *more* to your list?

If I am going to encourage you to do anything differently, I'll have to give you a few tips to energize yourself. I'm speaking more of the physical in this Simple Truth and the following ones. But from the physical comes the mental as the two are inextricably linked.

It's always seemed strange to me that fitness books aren't listed under self-help. I mean, isn't helping yourself the whole point of moving your body more? Of course, I'm not going to list exercises and the gyms nearest you, but I've always felt that getting to know your body was a great first step in getting to know yourself.

Note to Self:

From the physical comes the mental as the two are inextricably linked.

Simple Shift #13
Life is Just a Physics Equation
(Energy Out = Energy Back)

If you really stop to think about it, human beings are not so different from household appliances. We both perform various functions, we both have a certain life span, and we both use energy. Our toasters, coffeemakers, vacuum cleaners, and stereos use electricity; human beings require energy as well.

In fact, if we look at life in its simplest form, life really *is* just a physics equation:

$$Energy\ Out = Energy\ Back$$

In other words, if you don't expend much energy, you won't have much energy; if you don't put it out, you won't get it back. Think of a lazy Sunday spent on the couch, then analyze it a little more carefully. Do you spend six hours on the couch because you have no energy—or do you have no energy because you spent six hours on the couch?

Think of those Sunday afternoons a friend stopped by, dragged you off the couch, and took you to a local outdoor art show where you walked around for a few hours, smelling the fresh air, increasing your heart rate, and getting some sun on your face. Didn't you feel more energized and less tired when you got back home?

What about those weekends when you kept moving for some reason or other instead of sitting still? It might have been a drag to move your brother-in-law into his new apartment, but didn't you feel pretty good wiping the sweat off your brow and nursing those sore muscles later that evening?

The bottom line here is that you have to move your body more. (Well, unless you are a compulsive exerciser!) It's not even about losing weight or looking better at this point; it's about feeling better and having more energy by using more energy to feel better.

To do both, you need to get more oxygen in your bloodstream moving through your body. That's right; it's not just your lungs that need air—your entire body works better when it's infused with oxygen. If you are currently working at a job where you sit at a desk most of the day, then it is imperative that you move your body when you have a break. Coffee breaks were originally demanded by the labour movement. Key word there "labour," meaning those folks who work at physically demanding jobs need to sit down to re-energize themselves.

Physical labourers use break time to rest. For the rest of us, the opposite works best. If you're manning a desk seven hours a day, you need those break times for physical labour! Walk the stairs or grab a few co-workers and stroll the length of the parking lot and back. Move that body; it's better than a cup of coffee—and lasts loads longer!

You see, if you want to have more energy to enjoy your life more fully, the answer is simple: move your body! It's not a matter of choice. It really doesn't matter if you are a walker, a runner, a swimmer, a golfer, a biker, or a shopper. Just get that blood flowing. You will have more energy and will clear your head at the same time. Just a quick note about the added value of increasing your energy here with movement. More than half of your body is water, and energy flows best when we are well hydrated. You must drink ample amounts of plain water every day, somewhere between six and eight glasses of water and one extra glass for every cup of coffee you consume. Keep some by your side at all times.

SHIFT... OR GET OFF THE POT — 105

If you are a coffee drinker, have one in the morning and drink water the rest of the day. And *yes*, you will visit the toilet more times in the day, but hey, just think of the extra steps you are putting in. Cheers!

Note to Self:

You have to move your body more.

A Special Note on Footwear

The most important piece of equipment you require before beginning to exercise is proper footwear. Whatever the activity you are taking up—walking, running, basketball, biking, bird watching—you need a good, supportive, sports shoe.

This is where knowledgeable salespeople are worth their weight in gold. You need to find the store that fits your activity and find a professional who will assess your feet, so you get the shoe that will keep your knees, hips, and back healthy. Then spend a few bucks and tie them on.

Now you're ready to get your energy—and your life—back!

The Jump Test

"How comfortable are you in your own skin?"

It's a serious question. I often find that people with positive self-images move more, in fact, because *they are so positive*. It's not a big leap to consider the alternative: people with negative self-images move less because they figure, "Why bother?"

Which side of the spectrum do you fall on? Here's a test to see just how comfortable you are with your body. (You may want to ask a few family members or friends to gather around as support, but this is just for fun.)

Now remember, this is to see how comfortable you are in your own skin. This has nothing to do with shape, size, or weight.

Find a full-length mirror.
Take off all of your clothes.
Jump!
Time yourself to see how long it takes for things to stop jiggling...

If you are okay with the time, congratulations. You are comfortable in your own skin and have a great body image. Cheers. If you're like the rest of us, it may be time to move more, and jiggle less.

Note to Self:

I often find that people with positive self-images move more, in fact, because they are so positive.

Body Image: the Real Perspective

There is another way of looking at yourself that has more to do with the colours of the rainbow than the dark cloud of despair that always seems to follow you around. Most of us have a warped view of our body, but you can do a bit of reflective thinking to improve how you see yourself. Grab a piece of paper and jot down the answers to the following questions:

If you were to describe yourself in two colours, an inner colour and an outer colour, what would those colours be? The important part of this description is what those colours mean to you. For example, are you currently an "I have it all together" colour on the outside, and a fearful, insecure, "I have no idea what I'm doing" colour on the inside? Do you project a strong, unemotional persona on the exterior, while you know you are a teddy bear longing for comfort from other people on the inside? This next one might hurt: do you spend a lot of time, money, and energy on great hair, nails, and clothing but have not addressed why you are not comfortable in your own skin yet? Honestly, looking in the mirror takes courage and the truth is not always beautiful. Be honest and somewhat gentle with yourself as you start to move.

These discrepancies between inside and outside tell us something about our body image. When we can align who we really are both externally and internally, we can focus on the day-to-day tasks that make us more effective, while still being ourselves. We spend so much energy and time trying to be something we are not. Put that time and energy into your greater purpose, or at least go outside for a walk. For now, when in doubt about what to do with your increased energy, take yourself out for a walk.

Note to Self:

While most of us have a warped view of our bodies, you can do a bit of reflective thinking on how you see yourself— for the better.

What's in the tank today?

There is this misunderstanding about exercise that gives most of us an out from doing anything physical. We think, "If I don't have a good hour to get moving, why bother doing anything at all?"

Actually, what you want to ask yourself is: "What do I have in the tank today?"

See the small picture instead of the big; don't cop out because you can't run five kilometres today or bench press 280 pounds. Half a mile is better than no miles and 28 pounds is better than no pounds.

So don't ask yourself, "Why should I go to the gym if I only have fifteen minutes?" Instead, ask yourself, "What do I have in the tank today?"

"Five minutes? Ten? Can I get out there for an hour?"

If you decide, "Yes, I have enough for a thirty-minute walk," then walk out for 15 minutes and turn around. If you start out intending to go 30 and after five minutes, you think, "No way!" then turn around and simply be OK with it. You will find that no matter how much you put out there, when it comes to movement, anything at all will feel like you are *one-up* on the world. (If you like mornings and you get out for a walk or a run early, you really feel like you are playing hooky while the rest of your community sleeps. It's an awesome feeling!)

Now, don't misunderstand me here: you do get back what you put out there, so if your goal is to lose some weight, then the more you move and the higher the intensity, the better results you will get. But never underestimate the power of the five-minute blast. If you are going out for five minutes, make those five minutes worth every step.

We get too wrapped up thinking we have to be perfect

machines to exercise, complete with buckets of sweat and *Rocky* music in the background—nonsense. Fitness is incremental; our muscles grow over time, our bodies take shape based on what we do every day, not just a few times a week. Get in the habit of asking, "What do I have in the tank today?" and, increasingly, the answer will be more and more.

Note to Self:

You will find that no matter how much you put out there, when it comes to movement, anything feels like you are one-up on the world.

Aerobic versus anaerobic: what's the diff?

The definition of aerobic activity is "to use oxygen." It is activity that pushes you to increase your rate of breathing and heart rate. It is during aerobic activity that you will, in fact, burn stored body fat. This happens in your large muscles when fat cells are released into your bloodstream and metabolized (burned) with the oxygen you are breathing in and the water you are consuming.

You burn the most fat after the first 20 minutes of doing something aerobic. During the first 20 minutes of any aerobic activity, your body is basically using up any carbohydrates you have in it. (These are the easiest and fastest sources of energy your body will use to provide energy for the workout.)

Anaerobic activity is activity that builds muscle mass. Our body's metabolism is based on our lean body mass (muscles). Men have a naturally higher metabolism than women do and can therefore eat more in a day because they naturally burn it off. In order to have a higher metabolism, you need to do some resistance training, which will build up your body's muscles. This kind of activity also helps women fight the effects of osteoporosis and bone density loss.

To increase your body's natural metabolism, resistance training is a must. It's best to do some resistance muscle strengthening and then take the next day off to give your muscles a chance to rebuild. On your off days, that's when it's great to do some aerobic work.

Note to Self:

Recently I spoke in Chicago at a conference with Oprah's

trainer, Bob Greene. He reminded me that if you want to change your body, you must do something aerobic at least five or six days a week. There, I've said it.

Fitness Tip #1
Use the "don't think" method of exercise!

Much can be said about our ability to think and reason, but too often our heads get in the way of moving our bodies. The best advice I've ever received from a coach was to "stop thinking so much." Good advice we all should heed!

Scenario: You plan to go for a walk before work tomorrow morning. This requires you to wake up 30 minutes earlier than you are used to. Your alarm goes off, and your head kicks in, "I really could use an extra few minutes of rest; it rained last night and seems a bit cool outside this morning. My back is hurting. If I get into work a bit early, I'll finish some of that extra work I've been putting off. Blah, blah, blah."

Instead, blindly reach for your walking shoes, stumble from the bedroom and toward the front door, and repeat over and over and over, "Don't think, don't think, don't think…" all the way out the door.

Keep saying, "Don't think," all the way down the block, to the next one and the next, and by the time you get back home, you will have a smile on your face, some colour in your cheeks, and you will feel like you are one up on the world—because everyone else is still asleep. Remember that the body and mind are connected; know that the mental lift you get from getting more oxygen in your blood system is as beneficial as the physical lift you get from moving your body.

Note to Self:

Much can be said about our abilities to think and reason, but too often our heads get in the way of moving our bodies.

Fitness Tip #2
Always do something on a Monday!

Everything about us is determined by the habits of our daily lives. Right or wrong, it's the truth. If you were a fly on the wall of your life, you would see that you go through your day-to-day interactions with yourself, and others, *the same way every day.* Now, you might choose a different cereal on some days, or a different colour shirt, but generally you are who you are thanks to how comfortable you are with your routine.

When those habits result in a sedentary lifestyle, the only way to change our activity levels is to change our habits in the first place. One of the best tips I have ever heard for getting more active is this: *Always do something active on a Monday!* Because if you do something on a Monday, you will probably do it again on Wednesday, perhaps on Thursday, too, and maybe even on Saturday. If you wait until Wednesday, then Wednesday usually turns into Thursday, Saturday, next week or not at all.

Build better habits and you will build a better body; build a better body and along the way you will put out—and gain— more and more energy. Make energy your habit; make movement your habit. You don't have to start big, because any movement is usually an improvement over what we've done the day before.

Now, if you are reading this on any other day than a Monday, you simply must go out and do something active *today.* And then, make sure that next week you start your week being active on Monday!

Top Workout Tips

1. If you know you will be more apt to get out there if a buddy is going with you, then find someone to work out with and you'll keep each other on track.

2. Have your gear—shoes, shorts, sports bra, T-shirt—handy, so you don't have to *think* about it to put it on.

3. Have a bottle of water on hand at all times.

4. I work for myself, so I *never* take calls or book anything until after 9:30 each morning. As soon as I drop off my kids at school, I go right to my activity.

5. This is where some of you just had your "thinking" kick in. I felt it from where I'm sitting right now. "Oh, that's great for you Linda, but I work at a job that has me there from seven am until five pm… I only have half an hour for lunch. When am I supposed to eat? I have so much to do, groceries, making dinner, blah, blah blah"… Have I struck a chord yet?

6. If the only time you can move is at 6am before you go to work, or for 10 minutes at lunch, or at 8pm after all the dinner, homework and so on is complete, then that's when it's got to be.

7. *But wait, there's more!* Not moving your body is *not* an option. End of story; no discussion. Choose to get some movement in, however and whenever *you* define it.

Note to Self:

Everything about us is determined by the habits of our daily lives.

So always do something on a Monday!

Simple Shift #14
Find Your Own Funny Faster

"The art of medicine consists of keeping the patient amused while nature heals the disease."
~ Voltaire

Laughter isn't just the "best" medicine; it's also the most natural way to keep feeling energetic, healthy, and alive. When we laugh we feel more alive; you don't need to be a doctor to know that. But some amazing doctors have discovered some amazing ways in which laughter truly *is* the best medicine.

According to *HealthGuide.org*, "Laughter activates the chemistry of the will to live and increases our capacity to fight disease. Laughing relaxes the body and reduces problems associated with high blood pressure, strokes, arthritis, and ulcers. Some research suggests that laughter may also reduce the risk of heart disease."

The "funny" thing about laughter is, it can't just be a "one-time" thing; research shows that you must create what doctors call a "habit of humour" to attain the best health benefits. From *HealthGuide.org* again:

"Historically, research has shown that distressing emotions (depression, anger, anxiety, and stress) are all related to heart disease. A study done at the University of Maryland Medical Center suggests that a good sense of humour and the ability to laugh at stressful situations helps mitigate the damaging physical effects of distressing emotions."

So it's not just me telling you to laugh more; it's your doctors. Don't worry, you don't need a prescription to "find the funny faster," just a new outlook on life. And you're in luck, because that's definitely something I can help you with.

Note to Self:

When we laugh we feel more alive; you don't need to be a doctor to know that.

Tips for finding the funny faster

I have a pretty funny life although partly that's by accident: you can't live with the people I live with and *not* be funny (no offence). But what if you live alone, or if you're single or far away from your family and your workmates aren't exactly a laugh a minute? Don't worry; this list of five simple ways to "find the funny faster" will help you in your times of need.

1. **Humour is contagious:** The more you laugh, the more you want to laugh. If you know what makes you laugh, do more of it. If you're still experimenting, have fun doing it!

2. **Read:** We have lost touch with funny authors; everyone is so serious these days. Spend two hours on *Amazon.com* scoping out the hits you get from typing in the keyword "funny," spend twenty or thirty bucks, and I guarantee you'll find enough humour to keep you laughing for weeks on end!

3. **Surround yourself with humour:** Hang out with funny people; they are easy to spot because so many people are hanging around with them already!

4. **Choose funny first:** Seriously, how many "CSI"s do we really need? Watch TV any night of the week and it's murder, murder, murder. Change the channel until you find a good laugh track.

5. **Joke around:** Whatever happened to hearing, or telling, a good joke? Invest in a single joke book and I guarantee you, once you tell one joke, people will be dying to tell you three more.

Note to Self:

Humour is contagious: The more you laugh, the more you want to laugh.

The Queen of Laughter: may she rest in peace

I am a huge Erma Bombeck fan. I've read her books, scoured the Internet for all her old columns, and remind myself every day to embrace the small joys of life before it's too late. As Erma herself wrote not long after discovering she had cancer, "When I stand before God at the end of my life, I would hope that I would not have a single bit of talent left, and could say, 'I used everything you gave me.'"

Word to live by, folks, words to live by.

Erma was not just the "Queen of Laughter," as many have called her over the years, but she was also a true inspiration for women everywhere. She didn't climb mountains or jump from planes or hold public office, but quietly, with dignity, grace, charm and, of course, *humour* she made an impact on the planet that will be felt long after many of the rest of us join her at the great kitchen table in the sky.

In fact, the first book that I ever wrote was inspired by Erma because, even as I was procrastinating as I struggled with finishing that book, Erma passed away from cancer. I immediately said to myself, "Linda, get off your butt and finish this book."

At a funeral director's conference last year, we did an exercise where we put up humorous tombstones; this was to prove that you really *can* see the funny in everyday life. You just have to look for it – even in a cemetery. Not surprisingly, Erma Bombeck's tombstone was a gut-buster.

It simply said, "See, I told you I was sick."

Note to Self:

Find laughter in every day—even if it means writing your own funny tombstone!

Funny is in the ear of the beholder

Don't think you have to be Robin Williams, Joy Behar, or Jim Carrey to be funny; everyone has their own style of humour just as everyone has their own fingerprints. I've known people who were uproariously funny in a slapstick, trip-walking-through-the-door kind of way; I've also known people who were funny in a dry, witty, almost below-the-radar kind of way.

You know what? They were *all* funny in their own, unique way. The funny worked, no matter how it was achieved. I felt better; they felt better—we weren't worried about our ills or chills, at least not while we were laughing.

I'm sure you know people like this, too. The aunt who reads fine literature and sounds like an Oscar Wilde play, even when she's just doing the dishes. What about your geeky nephew who does the most amazing, hilarious dances in your living room? Or the spouse who has the uncanny ability to make you laugh in all kinds of situations

I believe even God has a sense of humour, and so do many religious leaders. How else can you explain the church sign I drove by the other day: "Having trouble sleeping? We have sermons; come hear one."

The point being that life is not about who frowns the most or who laughs most; it's about feeling good enough to serve your mission and accomplish your goals. Naturally, not every moment can be filled with laughter, but we can fill a lot more of them than we currently do, that's for sure!

I talked earlier about developing that "humour habit," but perhaps I misspoke. We don't really have to develop it so much as rediscover it. Remember when we were kids and we laughed, it seemed, all the time? We were on to something back then! Where did it go?

According to *Discovery Health*, "The average adult laughs about seventeen times a day. The average child laughs about three hundred times a day. Laughter not only releases 'mood-enhancing' endorphins but it actually burns about two calories per minute!"

Why let kids have all the fun?

Note to Self:

We all love to laugh. The most common feedback I get after a presentation is: "I haven't laughed that much and that hard in a long time." We need to get our laughter gusto back on track.

Simple Shift #15
Take Time to Get Quiet with Yourself and Turn Off the Noise

Remember when meditation was all the rage, and the most unlikely people went around sharing that telltale mantra: "Ommmmmmmmmmmmmmmmmm." We can look back and make fun now, but maybe we were really onto something back then.

I think the problem with meditation is that it quickly took on that New Age, hippy aspect and certain people took it to extremes, heading off to mountaintop ashram and quoting their gurus and generally nauseating the rest of us with their endless prattle. But you don't have to smoke anything or wear a loincloth to meditate; fact is, meditation is simply finding a few of the right times during your day to space out and break off from the daily grind that wears us down and saps the laughter from our very souls.

According to Lorin Roche, co-author of *Mediation 24/7: Practices to Enlighten Every Moment of Your Day*, "Just imagine... eating a simple meal and taking great delight in each bite, lying down and relaxing so deeply that in a few minutes you are rested and ready for action, walking and feeling the simple joy of movement as you stride along. Rich moments like these slip past people every day because they're too distracted, fatigued, or stressed-out to notice or enjoy them."

Doesn't sound so bad, does it? To me, it sounds pretty darn good. So break through the stigma and find the joys of meditation again. Still think you have to join a class, or go on a retreat, to meditate? Think again; here are five quick steps to blissful meditation:

1. **Treat it as a must-do, not a should-do:** Many of us start off with good intentions and quickly end with bad results merely because we lack the follow-through or motivation to stick with things. Meditation isn't about being hip or cool; it's about taking time for you and finding peace, however you define it. This is a necessity; we've already seen the many health benefits associated with decreasing stress through laughter and relaxation. Make it a habit, not a whim.

2. **Practice makes improvement:** I know it sounds like working at meditation would actually defeat the purpose. I mean, isn't this all supposed to be relaxing? Well, yes, it is, but we all know that people don't do quiet very well; it's a skill that takes practice so practice we must. Start slowly, with a few minutes each day. Concentrate on your breathing and what makes *you* relaxed versus what relaxes everyone else.

3. **Meditation = stillness:** Maybe what we're all hung up on is the word, "meditation." So find a new word: peace, serenity, calm, for example. What about stillness? That's a new concept, right? Not so much. At the last conference I attended, nearly every speaker mentioned the importance of stillness, of quieting the noise in your head. You can meditate in your office, on the elevator, in your car, in a busy mall. Stop equating meditation with hippies and gurus and make it more personally authentic and about finding your own inner stillness.

4. **Work up to at least ten minutes in a day:** I realize that's a tough thing for most people, but really just a few minutes of relaxation, mediation, or stillness is like a little exercise; it's better than nothing, but you have to get to a certain level of duration before it finally pays off.

5. **Never underestimate the importance of self-reflection:**
Once you have mastered the art of stillness—quieting the
noise inside your own mind—go to that next level and
really use this time each day to reflect on what you can do
to cut even more stress from your life. Self-reflection is
just that; reflecting on yourself. Not your job, not your
car payments, not your facial that afternoon.

Note to Self:

*Meditation isn't about being hip or cool; it's about taking
time for you and finding peace, however you define it.*

Simple Shift #16

The Power of Silence
A Grand Canyon Story

A few years back, Kevin and I decided we were going to take a few days away together. We thought we'd have a few days in Vegas combined with a quick trip to see the Grand Canyon. So we headed off to hike the canyon. When we arrived we were told by many not to hike down to the Colorado River and back on the same day. It's too hot and would be too tough to do it all in one day. But we had not planned ahead and booked a camping spot to allow us to spend a night down by the river. After a beer, we had a brainwave: we'd start really early, say about 4:30am and that way we could get down and back, we hoped, by nightfall the next day. Just a note to point out the average daily temperature had been reaching about +45 degrees Celsius, which is about 110 degrees Fahrenheit. Let's just say, "smoking hot!" So up we got at 4am to hit the trail by 4:30am. It was a beautiful 70 degree dawn of a day. We must have been about 35 minutes into the hike when I noticed something I had never noticed before. Nothingness, no noise, not even a breeze. No squirrels, no crickets, nothing. Just as I noticed the beauty of this amazing silence, the sun came up in the Grand Canyon about 5:07am and to say it was magical is putting it mildly. I have to say this moment was one of the most spiritual of my life. I did reflect later that we were, however, on our way down, and hoped that wasn't a sign.

Unfortunately, I have not had a similar experience since, but I have come to realize how critical turning off the noise in our daily lives really is.

As a speaker, I talk very quickly and have tried for years to slow down my rate of speech, but to no avail. Years ago, some colleagues suggested that instead of slowing down my rate of speech, I should just try and take more pauses. Now you have to know me to understand that I am very comfortable making people laugh, it's my fall-back mode of communication. It's the way I get comfortable when I feel insecure. But it took me about ten years into my professional speaking career to finally take that pause. One day, in front of about 400 people, I got to the point in my presentation where I was talking about taking some time each week to reflect and I took about a 45-second pause. And I, along with the other 400 people realized just how powerful silence can be. In fact I realized that silence is more powerful than when I have audiences laughing. But it makes us a bit uncomfortable so what do we do? We fill in the spaces with small talk, radio programs, TV shows, and so on. Distractions that allow us to avoid thinking about what's really going on in our heads and our hearts. So, I dare you to take some time this week to turn off the noise of your life and just see what comes up.

Note to Self:
Just get quiet and notice what you notice about yourself

Simple Shift #17

Two Hours Can Shift Your Life
Replenish Your Energy Bank

This chapter, hell, all of the second part of this book, is about energy. We have taken to thinking of "energy" as a quick fix, something we get out of a can or a bottle in one of those overpriced energy drinks. But this is a nickel-and-dime solution to energy depletion.

What if, deep inside you, you had an energy bank? What if your miraculous, beautiful, and self-healing human body had, deep within, all you need to have 365 energetic, powerful and meaningful days a year? What if you used to have the combination to the lock on this energy bank, but you've lost it somewhere along the way?

All of this is true, you know. Your body does have an energy bank, and from time to time you stumble across the combination—during a laughing attack, midway through or just after an intense workout, in moments of great stillness or peace—and tap into that energy bank and find yourself rejuvenated and alive.

Too quickly, however, you lose the combination and are right back to square one, running behind the eight ball and dogpaddling like crazy just to keep your head above water. Well, I'm here to tell you that the combination to that energy bank is closer than you think, all you need is two extra hours per day to find it.

Note to Self:
Love more of your days like it's a long weekend

The Real Simple Truth #1:
The Two Hours a Day That Will Change Your Life

Hold your horses, I know how it sounds—at first. "Two hours a day? Where the heck am I going to find two extra hours a day?" The trick is not to find extra time, but to rediscover how to spend your time more wisely.

Answer this question:

"If you were just given two extra hours in a day, and the time's not being taken away from anything else, it's a gift, and you cannot do *anything* job or career-related, what would you do with that time?"

Get at least five things down. Don't get logical. Just get them on paper.

This has to be pure "you time," whatever "you time" looks like to you. Some of you might read more, or sleep more, eat more, cook more, shop more, do your crafts, some art or even music, perhaps play with your kids or grandkids more. Hell, just get me outside more. Gardeners get your gloves! Maybe you would "fool around" more? I say sleep more! Whatever your "mores" are, if you have not done some of them in the past six weeks, who are you kidding? Start some of your mores today.

To help you answer that question, here are a few lines where you can jot down your answer:

_____

_____

_____

_____

_____

_____

One more caveat: you only have two minutes to decide what to do with those two hours. So, quick like a bunny, fill those lines in. I know, I know—two minutes isn't a whole lot of time, but you know what? This is kind of like those pop quizzes your teachers gave you back in school; you can't study or cram for this one. If you don't know the answers off the top of your head, all the time in the world isn't going to help you find them.

What, you still need help? That's fine; I'm going to throw some things out. The most important part of this is literally putting pen to paper, putting your thoughts in motion. Remember, this is a self-guided test, so here are some helpful questions from *me* to help *you* help *yourself*:

- Would you read more with those two extra hours?
- Would you sleep more?
- Would you eat more?
- Hang out with your friends more?
- Garden more?
- Play more music?
- Would you fool around more? (If so, what would you do with the other hour and 55 minutes?)

Okay, you get the point. So now go back, spend two minutes max, and write down what you would do with those two hours *if they were entirely yours to spend*.

In reality, most of us will spend our "more" time running extra copies instead of running a marathon, learning the latest sales figures instead of how to ride a jet ski or speak a foreign language, climbing the corporate ladder but not climbing the hill outside your back door.

So I ask again, "If you haven't done any of *your* mores in the last six weeks, then why is it that most of us will put between thirty-five or forty years into a job but no time into our mores?"

The answer is shorter than the question: it's because your job has gotten in the way of your life. *Your job has become more important than taking care of your own needs.* Those "mores" aren't extras, by the way, but interests and desires and hopes and dreams that are vital to your well-being.

We all think that we need to work so hard because the more hours we work the more money we make and the more money we make the more security we have and the more security we have the happier we'll be, but think about this: Is it really happiness if you can't even do the things that make you happy in the first place?

Do you think you'll have more time when you retire? Think again; you can't look at a newspaper, personal finance bestseller, or Internet site without finding out you need even more than "experts" first thought just to "survive" your golden years. There's a rosy thought, "surviving" your golden years. Sounds more like a prison sentence than a payoff.

Too often we think that spending time on ourselves is taking time away from our job, but just the opposite is actually true. If you do more of your "mores," you aren't neglecting your job, you're enhancing your work because this energizes you, gives you more creativity and time for thought, passion about life, and so on.

Spending more time on your "mores" isn't just a luxury or a bonus, it's part of the solution to your personal energy crisis. Remember what I said about energy? If not, here it is in a nutshell: energy is good for you! So what does that have to do with your list of "mores"? Simple: once you act on something—like learning to ride a jet ski or climbing a mountain—you get focused and your energy goes up. It's just simple physics

Bookmark this page; we're coming back to it.

Note to Self:

Move your body, breathe fresh air, be outside for some part of your day. Fresh air is pure energy; try walking outside—it's fast and easy.

Simple Shift #18
People, People, People
In the Big Picture, It's Only about People

Don't you know certain people who give you energy? Just thinking of them instantly revitalizes your spirit and puts a smile on your face. That *is* energy, my friend, maybe even the best kind.

Perhaps you're still thinking of energy as that juicy, sizzling stuff you get out of an energy drink or a caffeine pill or a triple espresso. The energy we get from genuine people and from trusting relationships with them is to energy drinks what Niagara Falls is to your bathroom tap; there's simply no comparison.

People fill us up with energy every day, all day. Just thinking about my sisters can cause my whole day to turn around; imagining my daughters coming home from school can make me an amateur race car driver to get home just to spend more time with them. This is energy you can't bottle, tag, or buy; you also can't live without it.

We have to be careful of the people we draw energy from: just as there is positive stress and negative stress, there are also positive relationships and damaging ones. Think of your boss: maybe she is a great gal, encouraging, nurturing, appreciative, and empowering. Yours is one great relationship. (Can you send her my resume?)

Now think of that "other" kind of boss or perhaps a coworker, the one who rides you all the time, cuts you down, questions your abilities, and makes you doubt yourself in places you didn't even think doubt could sprout. You end up spending all your time away from work worrying about your time at work. That is *not* the kind of relationship that gives you energy, and yet too often that is exactly the kind of person we spend most of our time with.

These negative influences can be your co-workers, your spouse, your child, your carpool driver or the cashier at your local coffee shop. It's okay to get rid of negative relationships and hold on to those we know to be powerful, sincere, and authentic. But don't misunderstand me: these are big decisions to make. So think them through. Just know that negative energy sappers can simply ruin your life, and at the very least, make your experiences less than optimal.

Relationships take maintenance; they don't maintain themselves. When we don't maintain our relationships very well, they can dwindle away until it's too painful, awkward, or just plain embarrassing to start them up again.

I used to think that exercise was more important than people on my list of where to spend time, but then I discovered that people who have strong, supportive relationships in their lives live longer, happier lives than a marathoner with no one.

Men and women maintain relationships differently, as we all know. Most men can phone up and talk to a friend they haven't seen in months and pick up right where they left off—no hidden agenda, no guilt, no expectations. Now, women have completely different expectations for relationships; we are closer, know more about each other, and we expect more. You can also hear us say things like, "Hmm, she hasn't called me in three weeks. I'm not calling her." Ahh—we're just different.

Note to Self:

Formula for a healthy life: we should all have one meaningful conversation per day. Stay in emotional contact with your friends and family.

Would you pass
"The Granny Rose Test"?

I had a few things going against me when I met my husband Kevin. He's the youngest son and grandson in a very large, Catholic, northern Canadian family. His mom and sisters are all great cooks and seamstresses, and when we first met, I had a bumper sticker on my Volkswagen Bug that said, "My Only Domestic Quality is I live in a House." To be honest with you, I was pretty proud about that fact. I am older than my husband and was well on my way in my career while he was still in college.

Fast forward a few years, and I finally got to meet his Granny Rose. Rose Sanderson was the matriarch of this family and held in high esteem. She was coming to his sister's house for Easter one year and I was to be presented. When I walked into Kevin's sister's home, there she was, surrounded by the family, everyone listening attentively. So I kept saying to myself, "Be gracious, Linda. Be a lady. Have some manners, you know the drill." I walked up to her and extended my hand and said something like, "Rose, it's a pleasure to finally meet you, Kevin just adores you and speaks very highly of you." She stood there, looked up at me, and very plainly stated, "You can't tell me you guys aren't sleeping together!" So I replied with "OK, let's colour some eggs…"

Ten years later, at the age of 97, Rose Sanderson passed away. Her small town of Fort Vermilion, Alberta, turned out to celebrate her life. Hundreds of people filled the only Catholic church in the town of just a few thousand. Her small home was filled with her family, friends, and townsfolk. My husband, his brother, and his cousin were asked to hand dig her grave, something my husband and I had never experienced. This experience proved to be profound for all of them as many townsfolk came by that morning to offer up hot coffee and observe the process. I was also asked to donate some makeup and hairspray to do Rose's hair and makeup, something else I'd never heard of. I remember asking Rose the last time I saw her, if she ever got lonely. She replied, "Are you kidding me? Look where I live. I live next to the post office. I am in my garden the very minute I can be in the spring and there till the snow flies in the late fall. Everyone gets their mail every day and everyone comes and visits me every day. I can't get any peace and quiet around here." To which I replied, "Good point."

As we view value in this crazy world of ours, I would have to say, on a world scale, Rose led a modest life. I remember driving away from her funeral thinking to myself, "What was that?"

A few years later I got my answer. At the time, I was the Director of the Run for the Cure Campaign and we had been given a large donation from a wealthy woman who lived about an hour south of our city. I had heard she originally wanted to give 2.5 million dollars to her local SPCA but her financial consultant had suggested she perhaps spread the dollars to a few organizations so many could benefit. So that's how we got our donation. I wanted to meet her and thank her personally so I drove down to see her. I had to ask her why she wanted to give all that money to the SPCA, and she replied without hesitation that she had received more affection from her dog than any other person in her life. Now as I drove away, I thought about Granny Rose who on a grand scale had seemed to have nothing, but really had everything. And this woman had all the wealth we all seem to want but *no* one to share it with.

Note to Self:

Nurture one person on your support network today. Buy a stamp and send them a handwritten letter. They will be shocked and very touched when they get the letter.

Section 3
When Was the Last Time You Did Something for the First Time?

Overview:
How Old are Your Stories?

OK, seriously, when you get together with your good friends, your buds, your peeps, your cronies or as I refer to mine, my DW40 club ("Desperate women over 40") how old are the stories you rehash as you relive the good ole days? Hey, no worries, we all do this. Sometimes it's a bridge back to a space where we can all get comfortable and there is definitely something to be said for that bridge. *But*, if your best stories are more than a decade old, and I'm going to assume that for some of you, your stories are a few decades old, then it's time to create some new stories. I think it's important at this juncture to point out that it is *not* those of us with the most "stuff" that win in the end, it's those of us with the best stories. It is so cool to feel eight years old again, that feeling that you had some courage to try something new but were still a bit afraid of the "what if?" You would forge ahead anyway and whamo, you'd get it. Now that's a cool feeling to recall, no matter what age you are right now. Start to think about some of the undones and what if's that you have bantered around in your brain for a few years, things that make you curious but scare you a bit too. This section of the book is dedicated to your rubber hitting the road of your life. Let's start with a simple assignment: I want you to consider planning a date for someone special in your life. Everyone loves

a surprise, even those of you who say, "I hate surprises."
Here's the bonus for you: planning something special for
someone in your life is as much for you as it is for them, because there is so much fun in the planning.

Note to Self:

*The next time you leave a building and a limo is sitting
there, if the people inside look OK,* get in! *It could be a great
story.*

Simple Shift #19
Check Your Judgments at the Door

Here's the short story on judgments; we all make them, all the time, and most of time, we are not even aware that we are doing it. It's our ego's way of staying strong. For some bizarre reason, we think we feel better when we judge others. What I am going to recommend here is this: For the sake of your own energy, just *notice* when you are making judgments. This will take some practice but what you will find is they (your judgments) are relentless. So give this a try for just a day to start, and when you catch yourself judging someone, or something else, just observe yourself doing it. That way you will create a space between who you really are and your subconscious mind. Once again, you will find yourself more in the moment. And your judgments will be "checked at the door."

Note to Self:
To judge others is a huge waste of energy and comes from a place of insecurity.

Simple Shift #20
Are You New Story-Ready?

Story-Readiness means feeling excited and challenged by change. Looking forward to new things and initiating it rather than simply reacting to events. Have you ever built an environment of trust and caring, going after resistance and charging people up? Now this takes some energy and how do we in today's age-diverse workplace take boomer and older work ethics and blend them with those of 20 year olds who are not as interested in working longer than a 40-hour work week? At the same time, how do we get these boomers to look at technology and fast-paced changes as positively as their younger colleagues?

To find out *your* story-ready strengths and weaknesses, how you deal with a world in constant flux, look over the following personal characteristics and see where your strengths and challenges lie. For this exercise, focus on your performance at work. You might want to do it twice, focusing the second time on your life outside of work to see if you change your responses. Then ask yourself why you are different at work and home? Something to ponder.

Rank yourself on the following traits on a scale of one to seven with one being low and seven being strong. Rank each trait on that scale.

Passion/Drive _____

If you have passion, nothing appears impossible. If you don't, change can be exhausting. Passion is the individual's level of personal fuel, intensity, and determination. You can feel some people's energy as it seems to ooze out of their pores. Let's pretend you have been given a daunting task at work and you know you are not qualified to do the job. Low scorers will feel worn out just looking at the task. Passionate people feel undaunted, perhaps even energized, which of course bugs their less than enthusiastic colleagues. Challenge kind of cranks them up. It has less to do with their ability than with enthusiasm and excitement. Their motto tends to be "what I lack in ability, I make up in determination."

Resourcefulness _____

Resourceful people are effective at making the most of any situation and using available resources to develop plans. They love making new connections and networks just so they can expand on who they know. They love the search. It's almost an erotic experience for them to go looking for the resources they need; they just like gathering information. They see more than one way to achieve a goal and they're able to look in less obvious places to find help. They have a real talent for creating new ways to solve old problems.

Optimism/ How you see what's ahead _____

Everyone has a pretty good sense of what this trait measures.

Do you have a positive view of the future? Do you see good things or more of the same? Some people say optimism can't be taught; it must be caught. Like a disease, you get it by hanging around the right people. While there's no denying that optimism is highly contagious, I believe there's more to it than that. You can train yourself to look for positives as well as negatives, but does what you see determine your attitude or does your attitude determine what you see? It works both ways. Optimism is a part of your frame of reference, which is made up of your past experiences, your belief systems, and your experiences of people and situations. All these things affect how you see your day, along with your outlook (optimistic or not). The good news is that you have control over this. Optimists tend to be more enthusiastic and positive about change. Their positive outlook is founded on an abiding faith in the future and the belief that things usually work out for the best, so they trust more.

Confidence

If optimism is the view that a situation will work out, confidence is the belief in your own ability to handle events, which again comes from past experiences. Many young people come off as if they are confident, but often this is what is called "false confidence." It's needed for a young adult to step into unfamiliar situations, but when we carry ourselves on false confidence for too many years, it turns into bravado and arrogance. There is *situational* confidence—"I know I can swim across this channel, learn this program, write this report"—and *self* confidence—"I can handle whatever comes at me." This latter type is the kind of confidence Change-Readiness is all about. But more specifically, self-confident people believe they can make any situation work for them.

One way or another they know they'll prevail, so they don't feel threatened by change. Another reason why change isn't forbidding to people high in confidence: they're unafraid of failing. Their self-belief is not based on a particular performance. Their ego and identity aren't on the line each time they go to bat. When they fail they don't see themselves as "a failure," but as a person who has something more to learn.

Adventurousness

"It's not the mountain you conquer, it's yourself"
—Sir Edmund Hillary

Two ingredients capture this adventurous spirit: the inclination to take risks and the desire to pursue the unknown, to walk the path less taken. Some people think you need courage to be adventurous, but the truth is you don't get courage until after you been on the adventure. Adventurous people love a challenge. They tend to be restless and shun the comfort zone. Routine bores them. They hate repetition and feel compelled to break out. They're always looking for new ways to do things. Adventurous people are great inventors and creators, pathfinders and scouts who go out ahead of the wagon train looking for opportunities and excitement. Some people who are highly adventurous, however, can also lean towards recklessness.

Adaptability

Adaptability includes two elements: flexibility and resilience. People who are adaptable invest less of their identity in the work they do or the function they perform. They tend to be highly self-aware individuals and know they are just part of the larger picture that is their experience. Flexibility involves ease of shifting expectations. If the situation changes, flexible people's expectations shift right along with it. They adjust to the new circumstances with quickness and ease, so they rarely feel disappointed or let down. Flexible people have goals and dreams like everybody else, but they're not overly attached to them. When something doesn't work out they'll say, "Plan A doesn't work; okay, let's look at plan B." They can go in many different directions and generally have a lot of options to work with. Resilient people aren't thrown by failure or mistakes. They don't dwell on them and get depressed but bounce back quickly and move on. Resilience is the capacity to rebound from adversity quickly with a minimum of trauma. Resilient people are nimble and fast on their feet.

Tolerance for the unknown

The one certainty surrounding change is that it spawns uncertainty. Now, for some personalities out there "order" calms them down so the "not knowing" in situations in their lives causes them much stress. For these folks, change is only a good thing when they themselves initiate it after they have had lots of time to think about its possible effects. No matter how carefully you plan it, there is always an element of ambiguity. You don't know what the competition is going to do or how the marketplace will respond. Sometimes solutions don't appear until well into the process, which is great unless you are a person who can't tolerate not knowing.

When things are vague, in flux, or unclear, people who are uncomfortable with ambiguity get impatient and irritable. On a deeper level, these folks fear others' discovering they are scared. So they come off as being bottom-liners, black and white thinkers. Without a healthy tolerance for ambiguity, change is not only uncomfortable, it's downright scary. But too much tolerance for flux can also get you in trouble: you may have difficulty finishing tasks and making decisions.

Scoring Yourself

You'll probably find you have higher scores on some traits and lower scores on others. Most people are like this and it means some people find it easier to create some new stories than others. The more you try new things on, the easier it is to step into the next new experience.

What are your strengths? Where do you need improvement? Are you surprised by any of your scores? You might find it interesting to have a friend, family member, or colleague rank you and see how they see you. The Creating New Stories quiz is also useful when coaching teams to determine which players to pick and what roles to put them in. Adventurers are great starters; resourceful people are excellent problem solvers; optimists make good cheerleaders, and their input is especially useful when people feel discouraged. Experiencing new things is an ongoing process. There is always room to grow and improve. One doesn't ever really stop expanding one's capacity to handle change, because quite frankly, "that's all there is folks." Change that is.

Note to Self:

The only constant we have come to know is change.

Simple Shift #21
The Mountain Theory of Goal Setting

I often tell to my audiences that I can't believe I am a speaker who talks about goal setting. Boring, boring, boring. My personality is a real squiggle, but I am a very ambitious person so the only way I get anything done is by compulsive goal-setting. While I was in labour with my first daughter, Chloe, I recall setting a goal to run a marathon. I figured, if I could do labour, I could do anything. It's funny what comes to your mind when your knees are up around your ears. So, after months of training I ran my first marathon. I had thought my goal was to run a marathon, but really it was to get back in shape after my first pregnancy. It turned into what has become a life-long adventure of experiencing sporting events. I have realized that the reason I go out several times a week to run, hike, walk, and so on, is to blab with good buddies. We have used events as an excuse for fun getaway weekends. More blabbing, accompanied by some wine drinking and good food eating. So if the goal was to get in shape, well perhaps I've accomplished that, but in reality I have reached a much deeper goal. The care and nurturing of friendships, the exercise of compassionate listening, the devotion to dreaming, and the occasional voice to tell a good pal to get over herself.

Now, for those of you who are more pragmatic in your thinking, let me give you my scientific version of the Mountain Theory of Goal Setting:

1. You start at the bottom of the mountain looking up at your goal, which would be the top.

2. You set out on your journey to the top and get several hundred feet toward the peak.

3. Along the way you might meet people who give you some advice as to which trail is better or more challenging. You take that into consideration.

4. At some point about halfway up, you find a vista to enjoy the amazing view and you notice a beautiful lake off in the distance. You didn't even know that this lake existed until this moment, because when you were just starting out on your journey, you couldn't see the lake since the mountain was in the way.

5. So you decide, hey, I love that lake, and you head off toward it to spend some time. Once you get there, while enjoying the spectacular view, you remember you never did learn how to swim, so you head back to town to take some swimming lessons at the local Rec Centre. Now while you are there, you meet this cute lifeguard and start to date, eventually get married, and never head back to the mountain. Well, maybe the two of you head back to the mountain or perhaps you both go and build a house on that lake, or who knows, you might both decide to fly across the planet and start up a new Rec Centre together somewhere else.

6. So here's the deal: you won't find out what the goal is until you are in the middle of going after it. The point is JUST START... and see where it takes you.

Note to Self:

Take swimming lessons before you take up hiking mountains.

Simple Shift #22
Don't Think, Don't Think, Don't Think!

Back in "Simple Shift #13," I wrote about not allowing your head to kick in when you want to do something for yourself like exercise. But the "Don't Think" method of getting stuff done also applies to several other aspects of our lives. Our minds/egos do everything they can to hold us back from really becoming ourselves. It's critical, judgmental, and measures all of our accomplishments and goals against the world out in front of us.

So as you think about those things you want to accomplish this year and in those two extra hours in a day, use the "Don't Think" method to just move on them. Get something started. It's all physics. It's inertia and once you get the ball moving, it rolls along with ease and grace. What is very interesting to observe about yourself is when your brain starts to do its thing, (think, judge, criticize) just start to notice that is what you are doing. Starting to observe yourself in these instances creates some space where you can bring yourself into the present moment. And it's in the present moment that we hold our power, our creative thought, and our passion to move on the goals that add the good spices to our lives. So "Don't Think!" and "Move on Your Undones" this year.

Note to Self:

Don't let your head get in the way of what your heart wants to do.

Simple Shift #23
Take an Honest Snapshot of Your Life
Measure the Balance in Your Life

It seems funny that I am asking you to take a snapshot of your life right now, when we are so close to the end of this book. But because the picture you are about to reveal is an ever-changing photo, whenever you take this shot is perfect. Below you will find a survey of where you find yourself spending time. Here is how you are to rank yourself. I always suggest you be honest with yourself or the survey is basically a waste of your time. Here's some colour commentary on how you rank yourself:

"A" means you are really winning in this part of your life.

"B" means you are doing pretty well here but there is a bit of room for improvement.

"C" means you are doing OK but there is a lot of room for improvement.

"D" means you are in denial and basically ignoring this part of your life.

Rank yourself in the following areas:

A = Very Satisfied
B = Satisfied
C = Dissatisfied
D = Very Dissatisfied

Health	A	B	C	D
Physical Activity	A	B	C	D
Your Body	A	B	C	D
Mental	A	B	C	D
Food and Nutrition	A	B	C	D
Career	A	B	C	D
Finances	A	B	C	D
Personal Development				
(intellectual)	A	B	C	D
Community				
Involvement	A	B	C	D
Relationships	A	B	C	D
Spirituality	A	B	C	D
Home	A	B	C	D
Play and Recreation				
(attitude)	A	B	C	D

Note to Self:

Start spending time in a few areas of your life that need some attention and energy

Simple Shift #24
Personal Accountability Made Easy

There are probably two things to be said about being human. Number one: although we are all different, we are very predictable. Number two: If we can find a way to procrastinate on something, we will. Even those of you who are sitting reading this saying to yourself, "Heck, I never procrastinate on anything," secretly wish you could allow yourself some latitude to procrastinate. You just judge yourself and others so harshly that it's not an option. But for the other 99% of us, procrastination is the best way to make some space for ourselves right now.

So if we are clear that most of us do procrastinate. Here's what I'm going to propose: a few years back, I co-authored a workbook on accountability called *Guilt Free Accountability: The Official Guide to Becoming Bold, Adventurous, and Gutsy*. Through the process of encouraging folks from all across North America to become accountable for their own happiness, it very quickly became clear that when we set out some goals, write them down, and share them with a few people, magic starts to happen. Now the interesting thing is, once we start to write things down, we increase our chances of actually doing anything about these items to about 50/50, even if we don't look at them again. And if you tell someone what you want to accomplish, your raise your chances to act on these goals to about 80%. But fewer than 4% of us ever write a darned thing down outside of our working lives, let alone tell someone what we are dreaming about. This is because these notes we make become our mirrors to ourselves and most of us hate looking in the mirror. Also, we actually believe that those who we might tell about our goals will actually judge us if we don't accomplish them. The truth is, no one is really ever thinking about *you* because they spend most of their time worrying what others are thinking about *them*.

But here's what really happens when we make some goals: we think about them, write them down, and tell someone, and then things just simply start to happen. Yes indeed, the universe collides to move you closer toward your dreams, goals, and undones. An energy carries you further than you can imagine, and you start to reach your goals much faster than you expected. You then find yourself sitting and thinking, "Well, that happened pretty fast...now what?" It's the "now what?" that scares the hell out of us, but what we realize is we now have to move the goalposts further out. That takes energy, and most of us would rather just hover where we are because for most of us, where we are is pretty darned good. But what I have discovered is that all of us have some burning dreams and gut urges to try something new this year, this month, today. So the bottom line here is to get your thoughts on paper, share them with someone you feel comfortable with, and take one small step toward it. Just see how charged up you will get.

Note to Self:
- *Think it*
- *Write it down*
- *Tell someone what you want to do*

Simple Shift #25
What Does There Look Like?

Recognizing and Celebrating Life's Benchmarks and Milestones

Although the above question is an odd one, I like it. I was inspired to write about it, and plan to do extensive research into it for my next book, because I am married to a very driven businessman. Kevin owns his own development and construction company and currently has about 50 staff and several other contract suppliers. He works incredibly hard and I often ask him what drives him. We live on beautiful acreage in the Okanagan Valley, with all the toys and stuff one could ever need. I just like to put it this way: we live a busy, large life, but both of us continue to drive forward going after something. The question I ask not only myself and my family, but you too is, "Do you know what *there* looks like?" and if you do, are you able to celebrate some of the successes along the way?

This chapter is dedicated to helping you define for yourself what *there* means to you and give yourself permission to be grateful and proud of your success to date and to come.

Have you ever asked yourself if you have arrived yet? What I want you to do is go back to "Simple Shift #2," and revisit your top values. Do you find that, for the most part, you make your work and home life decisions based on what is important to you? As you reflect on this, I want you to sit for a moment and close your eyes. Imagine you could design your own "it doesn't get any better than this!" day.

See it in your mind's eye from waking up to going to bed that night. Then I want you to write down on paper what it looks like. What does it taste like? What does it feel like, smell like? Get as detailed as you can with your description so you can almost see it. Now as you imagine this day, it's important to notice how your body feels in it. After you have gotten all the details down on paper, take a moment and look at the day you have just created and see if there are any themes that jump out at you. Does this day incorporate your top five values as you defined them earlier in the book, or is it a design of something completely different? I doubt that it will be different, but thought I should ask.

Thinking about the elements of your perfect day, are you currently living and designing your life with those elements in it. You see, you do not have to be wealthy to be *there*. But you do need to recognize what you value. You must also be able to recognize when some of these elements present themselves to you in the coming years. We simply must stop, pay some recognition, and be grateful. I am guessing that most of us have some of *there* in our lives every day, but we focus on what's not *there*. If you have some *there* descriptions you want to share with me for my research, I would love for you to send them to me. *info@lindaedgecombe.com* "What does *there* look like for you?"

Note to Self:

Send Linda your definition of there. *info@lindaedge-combe.com*

Simple Shift #26
Final Commitment

I wanted to share this last piece with you because for the past several years I have been doing research on how to get people committed and accountable to themselves. What I have found is a very simple process to help people start to do the things they really want to do. So, with that in mind, your final commitment to me is sending me an email telling me about at least one thing you have started, inspired by this book. Even if you haven't started or done anything from reading this book, you still have to email me.

This one simple act of emailing someone with your dreams, goals, and desires, is the catalyst everyone needs. All I can say is, trust me on this one. You will see for your-self: the increase in energy, self-esteem, humour, and health you will get from just *moving* on something that you value.

I look forward to your email and I will respond to you.

Email me at: *info@lindaedgecombe.com* or visit my site and email me from it at: *www.lindaedgecombe.com*

All the best in Shifting to get your life back.

Linda Mae

About Linda

Linda Edgecombe, BPE. Best-Selling Author,
Award Winning Speaker,
Certified Speaking Professional (CSP), Humorist,

"Life Accountability and Perspective Specialist"

Linda Edgecombe, CSP is an internationally renowned award-winning humorous speaker, trainer and consultant. She is a best-selling author who energizes every room as she leads people to loosen up, lighten the load and laugh. Her audiences are motivated and shown how they can shift their perspectives on life, work and themselves. Change has never been this painless!

As a professional, with a degree in Physical Education, Linda brings 20+ years of Recreation, Employee Wellness, Lifestyle and Corporate Consulting experience to her programs and her clients. She was a consultant for PARTICI-PACTION promoting healthy living to Canadians and is known for being one of the country's most popular Speakers. Most recently featured in the *Wall Street Journal* as an expert in "Shifting Perspectives".

Inside all the laughter, Linda's audiences are inspired to find the meaning in what they do and let go of what's not working. Her message is a welcome as a deep belly laugh and as profound as an honest look in the mirror.

You Find out more about booking Linda at:

Learning Edge Resources
"Accountability with an Edge"
www.lindaedgecombe.com
info@lindaedgecombe.com
1-250-868-9601